The Bible's Greatest Hits

The Bible's Greatest Hits

Top Sixty-Six Passages from Genesis to Revelation

Henry G. Brinton

RESOURCE *Publications* • Eugene, Oregon

THE BIBLE'S GREATEST HITS
Top Sixty-Six Passages from Genesis to Revelation

Copyright © 2021 Henry G. Brinton. All rights reserved. Except for brief quotations in critical publications or reviews, no part of this book may be reproduced in any manner without prior written permission from the publisher. Write: Permissions, Wipf and Stock Publishers, 199 W. 8th Ave., Suite 3, Eugene, OR 97401.

Resource Publications
An Imprint of Wipf and Stock Publishers
199 W. 8th Ave., Suite 3
Eugene, OR 97401

www.wipfandstock.com

PAPERBACK ISBN: 978-1-6667-0586-7
HARDCOVER ISBN: 978-1-6667-0587-4
EBOOK ISBN: 978-1-6667-0588-1

06/21/21

Unless otherwise noted, Scripture quotations are from the New Revised Standard Version Bible, copyright © 1989 National Council of the Churches of Christ in the United States of America. Used by permission. All rights reserved worldwide.

Dedicated to

Members of my Bible Studies at
Sixth Presbyterian Church, Washington, DC
First United Church of Christ, Milford, Connecticut
Calvary Presbyterian Church, Alexandria, Virginia
Fairfax Presbyterian Church, Fairfax, Virginia

"In the beginning was the Word . . ." (John 1:1)

Contents

Introduction | ix

1. Genesis 1:1—2:4 | 1
2. Exodus 14:5-31 | 4
3. Leviticus 19:1-18 | 7
4. Numbers 21:4-9 | 10
5. Deuteronomy 6:1-9 | 13
6. Joshua 3:7-17 | 16
7. Judges 4:1-10 | 19
8. Ruth 1:1-18 | 22
9. 1 Samuel 17:32-49 | 25
10. 2 Samuel 11:1-15 | 28
11. 1 Kings 19:1-15 | 31
12. 2 Kings 2:1-12 | 34
13. 1 Chronicles 4:1-10 | 37
14. 2 Chronicles 36:15-23 | 40
15. Ezra 3:1-13 | 43
16. Nehemiah 8:1-10 | 46
17. Esther 7:1-10 | 49
18. Job 38:1-7 | 52
19. Psalm 23 | 55
20. Proverbs 8:1-31 | 58
21. Ecclesiastes 1:1-14 | 61
22. Song of Solomon 2:8-14 | 64
23. Isaiah 56:1-8 | 67
24. Jeremiah 31:31-34 | 70
25. Lamentations 3:22-33 | 73
26. Ezekiel 37:1-14 | 76
27. Daniel 7:9-14 | 79
28. Hosea 1:2-10 | 82
29. Joel 2:1-17 | 85
30. Amos 5:18-24 | 88
31. Obadiah 10-16 | 91
32. Jonah 3:1-10 | 94
33. Micah 5:2-5 | 97
34. Nahum 1:1-11 | 100
35. Habakkuk 1:1-4; 2:1-4 | 103
36. Zephaniah 3:14-20 | 106
37. Haggai 1:14—2:9 | 109
38. Zechariah 9:9-12 | 112
39. Malachi 3:1-4 | 115
40. Matthew 22:34-40 | 118
41. Mark 16:1-8 | 121
42. Luke 4:14-21 | 124
43. John 3:14-21 | 127
44. Acts 2:1-21 | 130
45. Romans 4:1-25 | 133
46. 1 Corinthians 13:4-8 | 136
47. 2 Corinthians 5:16-21 | 139
48. Galatians 3:23-29 | 142

49	Ephesians 4:25—5:14 | 145		59	James 5:13–20 | 175
50	Philippians 2:5–11 | 148		60	1 Peter 2:19–25 | 178
51	Colossians 1:15–23 | 151		61	2 Peter 3:8–15 | 181
52	1 Thessalonians 5:16–24 | 154		62	1 John 4:7–21 | 184
53	2 Thessalonians 2:1–17 | 157		63	2 John 4–11 | 187
54	1 Timothy 1:12–17 | 160		64	3 John 1–8 | 190
55	2 Timothy 4:6–8, 16–18 | 163		65	Jude 3–13 | 193
56	Titus 3:1–7 | 166		66	Revelation 21:1–4; 22:1–7 | 196
57	Philemon 1–21 | 169			
58	Hebrews 9:23–28 | 172			*Epilogue* | 199
				Bibliography | 201

Introduction

IN 1976, THE EAGLES released *Their Greatest Hits (1971–1975)*, and it became one of the most popular albums of all time, selling over 42 million copies. "One of These Nights" and "Best of My Love" are songs on the album that topped the singles charts, along with classics such as "Take It Easy" and "Desperado." About the same time, Elton John released his *Greatest Hits*, spanning the years 1970 to 1974. Containing songs such as "Daniel" and "Bennie and the Jets," it turned into the best-selling greatest hits album by a solo artist, with 24 million copies sold worldwide. Greatest hits albums remained popular through the 1990s, but then music streaming services made it easier for fans to listen to their favorite tunes. Now, anyone can simply ask Alexa for their favorite artist's greatest hits, and the music will be automatically delivered.

But what are *the Bible's* greatest hits? Study guides have been written about entire books of the Bible, or about sections of Scripture such as the Gospels or the biblical prophets. But no list has ever been compiled of the greatest passages from all sixty-six books of the Bible. Perhaps people have been reluctant to identify the "classics" of Holy Scripture because they see value in larger sections of the Bible, or because they sense that people of faith are not going to be in agreement about which passages should top the biblical "singles charts." Such concerns are certainly legitimate. If the creation story from Genesis is selected as the best of this particular book, what about the Great Flood or God's covenant with Abraham? Bible readers are not going to be in harmony about these selections, just as music fans are going to argue about why "Tiny Dancer" and "Levon" did not make it on to Elton John's *Greatest Hits*.

Disagreements are part of the fun, however, and lively discussions can draw people into deeper appreciations of the breadth of both pop music and Holy Scripture. My hope is that this book will stimulate spirited discussions about the passages that have been selected, and will lead to talk about other important biblical stories as well. An individual can read this book in its entirety as a private exercise and gain insights into the significant passages that appear in biblical books that are often overlooked and unread. It can also be used by a Bible study class in a week-by-week discussion format, with conversations guided by the questions that are included at the end of each chapter. The first draft of the book was used in the Basic Bible class of Fairfax Presbyterian Church, where I serve as pastor, and it led to numerous group discoveries over the course of several years. Many of the biblical insights and contemporary applications in the book have been shared in sermons I have preached in Fairfax and been published in the preaching journals *Homiletics* and *Proclaim*. By the end of the book, I hope that every reader will have gained a new appreciation for the greatness of the numerous passages that fill the Bible from beginning to end.

Each of the sixty-six chapters in this book is short and high-impact, like a top single on the radio. For readers who want to go broader and deeper, I recommend Tyler D. Mayfield's *A Guide to Bible Basics* (Louisville: Westminster John Knox, 2018), which has been an excellent guidebook for me. An understanding of the Hebrew Scriptures can be enhanced by Walter Brueggemann's *An Introduction to the Old Testament* (Louisville: Westminster John Knox, 2003). For those who want an outstanding series of biblical commentaries, I recommend *The New Interpreter's Bible* (Nashville: Abingdon), which was published in twelve volumes beginning in 1994. My hope is that my book will inspire an interest in biblical studies that will lead to more in-depth examinations of all of the books of Holy Scripture—from the well-known to the obscure.

For now, let the discussions and debates begin. Here come *The Bible's Greatest Hits: Top Sixty-Six Passages from Genesis to Revelation!*

Henry G. Brinton
Occoquan, Virginia

1

Genesis 1:1—2:4

THE FIRST BOOK IN the Bible is all about beginnings. *Bereshit* is the first Hebrew word in the book, translated into English as "in the beginning," which gives the book its name in the Jewish tradition. When the Hebrew Bible was translated into Greek, the book was called *Genesis*, which means "origin," a name which continues to be used in our English Bibles. Genesis is the origin story for the entire spiritual adventure that follows, from the creation of the heavens and the earth (Gen 1:1) to the arrival of a new heaven and a new earth (Rev 21:1).

The book begins with God creating the universe when "the earth was a formless void and darkness covered the face of the deep" (Gen 1:2). God did not create the universe out of nothing, but instead made it out of a dark, formless, watery, and chaotic space—something we might imagine as swirling gas or liquid. Genesis makes clear that God was distinct and entirely separate from creation, saying that "a wind from God swept over the face of the waters" (Gen 1:2). The Hebrew word for "wind" is *ruah*, which can also be translated "spirit" or "breath." While we English speakers feel the need to use different translations of this word in different biblical stories, the word in Hebrew is the same. It reminds us that God's Spirit can come to earth as a mighty wind, such as on the Day of Pentecost (Acts 2:1–4), or in a gentle breath, as when Jesus breathed on the disciples and said, "Receive the Holy Spirit" (John 20:22).

On the first day, God created the powerful light that is absolutely essential for life, using only the words, "Let there be light" (Gen 1:3). God saw that the light was good, and then God separated the light from the darkness. God used a set of words to bring order out of chaos—creative speech that God has continued to offer through all of history. God has continued to speak through the words of the prophets, through the preaching of apostles, and most powerfully through the teachings of Jesus: the Word of God in human form (John 1:14). In the chaos of twenty-first century political posturing and cultural conflict, we need these divine words more than ever.

In my novel *City of Peace*, a Methodist pastor named Harley Camden speaks about the power of words. "I'm convinced that words create reality," Harley explains. "It's a very biblical idea. Think of God creating the world in Genesis, saying 'Let there be light,' and there is light. Jesus is described in the New Testament as 'the Word.' When Martin Luther King Jr. said, 'I have a dream,' people began to see a vision of a new world of equality. Words create reality. Whether we say 'I love you' or 'I hate you' makes a huge difference."[1]

Words are critical to the creative work of God. This continues on the second day of creation, when God said, "Let there be a dome in the midst of the waters, and let it separate the waters from the waters" (Gen 1:6). We may wonder about this talk of a "dome" that separated the waters underneath from the waters above, because we know from the work of NASA that there is, in fact, no dome above us in the sky. But the writers of Genesis based their words on what they observed, and when they looked up they saw a blue dome. This barrier kept the waters above the dome from falling to earth, except when "the windows of the heavens were opened," as they were in the Great Flood (Gen 7:11). Even today, we adopt this ancient understanding when we look outside at pouring rain and say, "The heavens have opened."

On the third day, God spoke the Seas and Earth into being, and out of the Earth came vegetation. God saw that these developments were good. From the very beginning of the Bible, the world is described as fundamentally good in every dimension—from fruit seeds to human bodies. As a result, people of faith are invited to see the world and life itself as good gifts of God, instead of being suspicious or distrustful of what God has created. On day four, God made lights in the dome of the sky, and then on the fifth day was the creation of creatures in the waters, birds, and sea monsters. On the sixth day, God created cattle, creeping things, and wild animals. Then God said, "Let us make humankind in our image, according to our likeness

---

1 Brinton, *City of Peace*, 227.

... So God created humankind in his image ... male and female he created them" (Gen 1:26–27).

Finally, on the seventh day, God finished the work of creation by resting. God took a Sabbath day and instructed us to do the same—to cease our work, to rest, to recover, and to remember that our value comes not from what we *do*, but from who we *are*—creatures made in the image of God. Genesis is all about beginnings, from God's word that created light to God's rest that established the Sabbath. The creation story is the first of the Bible's greatest hits because it tells us that God has made a world for us to enjoy, full of things that are not just good, but "very good" (Gen 1:31).

Questions:

1. How do words create reality for you?
2. Where do you see goodness in God's creation?
3. What does the sabbath mean to you, and how do you observe it?

2

Exodus 14:5–31

AT THE HEART OF the Book of Exodus is the story of the Israelites escaping Egyptian bondage. This story is central to Jewish faith and identity, remembered each year in the celebration of Passover. The word *exodus* is from Greek and means "going out"—that is, going out of captivity in Egypt. The promise of the book is that oppressive empires are no match for the power of a just and loving God.

Exodus links religious faith to the work of liberation and stresses God's love for the oppressed of the earth. This approach inspired abolitionists to fight slavery in the nineteenth century and Civil Rights leaders to work for racial justice in the twentieth. But "the message of liberation is always a tough sell," I wrote in my book *Balancing Acts*, "because it requires a departure from tradition and a journey to a new place."[1] Exodus is not about preserving tradition and maintaining the status quo, but about moving toward the Promised Land and becoming the people that God wants us to be.

The story begins after ten plagues were sent by God to the Egyptians, including the death of all the firstborn in the land. As a result, the Egyptians urged the Israelites to depart. But when Pharaoh learned that the people had fled, he and his officials had a change of heart, and they said, "What have we done, letting Israel leave our service?" (Exod 14:5). They did not want to lose their cheap and plentiful slave labor, which had made them rich and powerful.

---

1. Brinton, *Balancing Acts*, 10–11.

Exodus 14:5–31

When the Rev. Dr. Martin Luther King Jr. wrote his *Letter From Birmingham City Jail*, he said, "We know through painful experience that freedom is never voluntarily given by the oppressor; it must be demanded by the oppressed. Frankly, I have never yet engaged in a direct action movement that was 'well-timed,' according to the timetable of those who have not suffered unduly from the disease of segregation. For years now I have heard the words 'Wait!' It rings in the ear of every Negro with a piercing familiarity. This 'Wait' has almost always meant 'Never.'"[2] Freedom was not voluntarily given by Pharaoh, nor is it given by oppressors today. In unjust societies, the word "wait" almost always means "never."

Exodus tells us that God "hardened the heart of Pharaoh king of Egypt and he pursued the Israelites, who were going out boldly" (Exod 14:8). When the Israelites looked back, they saw the Egyptians advancing and complained to Moses, "it would have been better for us to serve the Egyptians than to die in the wilderness" (Exod 14:12). In their fear and panic, they jumped to the conclusion that being slaves in Egypt would be better than dying in the desert.

But the fear of the people was not all bad, since it positioned them to put their trust in the power of God. "Do not be afraid," said Moses, "stand firm, and see the deliverance that the LORD will accomplish for you today; for the Egyptians whom you see today you shall never see again. The LORD will fight for you" (Exod 14:13–14). The command of Moses, "Do not be afraid," along with the closely related phrase "Have no fear," is the most commonly repeated phrase in the whole Bible, appearing approximately eighty times in both the Old Testament and the New Testament. This command is grounded not in wishful thinking, but in the conviction that Almighty God is willing to fight for God's people.

The Israelites were challenged to look forward in faith instead of back in fear. God told them to go forward, and God instructed Moses to stretch out his hand over the sea and divide it, so that the Israelites could walk into the sea on dry ground. Reaching the shoreline, Moses stretched out his hand, and God drove the sea back, divided the waters, and turned the sea into land. The Israelites then crossed the sea on dry ground, with the waters standing as walls on either side of them. When the waters returned and drowned the Egyptians, "Israel saw the great work that the LORD did against the Egyptians. So the people feared the LORD and believed in the LORD and in his servant Moses" (Exod 14:31).

2. King, "What Dr. King Wrote," 30.

At the end of the story, the people "feared the LORD" and believed in both God and Moses. The words "feared" and "believed" are both significant, even though the phrase "fear of the LORD" has fallen out of usage in recent years. This is unfortunate, because fear is a feeling of profound respect that comes when we see God bring order out of chaos, healing out of illness, and justice out of injustice. Such a God deserves our fear as well as our belief—our profound respect as well as our trust. The Exodus story is one of the Bible's greatest hits because it shows us the power of God to overcome daunting obstacles and lead us to new life. Oppressive forces—whether political or spiritual—are no match for the power of our just and loving God.

Questions:

1. When have you seen oppressed people trusting the power of God?
2. How does your faith carry you forward in dangerous times?
3. What does it mean to you to "fear the Lord"?

3

Leviticus 19:1–18

The Book of Leviticus gets its name from the Levitical priests who served as leaders of religious services among the people of Israel. Leviticus contains a mix of religious, civil, and moral regulations, and at the heart of the book is chapter 19, which contains rules about holiness—especially holiness in social ethics. Although people today are often suspicious of the word "holy," with self-righteous individuals being accused of acting "holier-than-thou," "holy" is a very positive term in Leviticus. Holiness is the central characteristic of God, and it has multiple meanings for the people of Israel: separateness, righteousness, justice.

The chapter begins with God saying to Moses: "Speak to all the congregation of the people of Israel and say to them: You shall be holy, for I the Lord your God am holy" (Lev 19:2). Because God is holy, the people of Israel are to be holy—separate from people around them, and both righteous and just in their dealings with one another. Chapter 19 addresses holiness in family relationships, sacrifices, farming, and business, and in the eighteenth verse of the chapter, love of neighbor becomes central to a life of holiness.

"You shall each revere your mother and father," says God to the people, "and you shall keep my sabbaths: I am the Lord your God. Do not turn to idols or make cast images for yourselves" (Lev 19:3–4). These two verses are similar to the Ten Commandments—rules about revering mother and father, keeping the sabbath, and avoiding idols. Holiness begins with revering mother and father: the people who have given life to their children. Sabbath-keeping is commanded as well—a practice that was instituted in

Genesis 1 and appears frequently in the Old Testament: fifteen times in Exodus, twenty-four times in Leviticus, and sixty-seven times in the rest of the Old Testament books. The sabbath reminds us that our value comes from who we are as children of God, not from what we do as workers in the world. Unfortunately, our Internet-connected global economy keeps us focused on work every day of the week.

This industriousness can tip over into idolatry, which happens when we put more emphasis on money, possessions, sex, or success than we do on God. "Popular television shows contain a lot of sin," I wrote in a column for *USA Today*, "but even more idolatry." In *House of Cards*, the idol is power. Conniving politician Frank Underwood schemes and sleeps his way through Washington, moving from Democratic majority whip to vice president to president.

Mad Men idolizes success. Suave 1960s advertising man Don Draper, who reinvents himself throughout the series, believes that "success comes from standing out, not fitting in." Unfortunately, his "standing out" does terrible damage to his family members, friends, and colleagues.

Surprisingly, the idol of the drama *Breaking Bad* is family. After being diagnosed with cancer, chemistry teacher Walter White builds a drug empire on the belief that he needs to provide for his wife and children. But even a good thing can cause death and destruction once it becomes an idol. At one point, Walt's wife says, "Someone has to protect this family from the man who protects this family."

Idolatry is nothing new, of course. Leviticus warned against idolatry, and Protestant reformer John Calvin wrote that human nature "is a perpetual factory of idols," an observation that continues to ring true as people make idols of sex, power, beauty, success, money, and even children. None of these is inherently evil, but they become sinful when they are treated as divine.[1]

Leviticus goes on to offer a number of laws on community and social morality, demanding honesty and justice in dealing with others. In echoes of the Ten Commandments, God says, "You shall not steal; you shall not deal falsely; and you shall not lie to one another. And you shall not swear falsely by my name" (Lev 19:11–12). Also forbidden are unjust judgments, partiality toward the poor, and deference to the powerful. Slander is prohibited, as is hatred, vengeance, and the bearing of grudges. The section ends with a commandment that identifies love as the organizing principle

---

1. Brinton, "False idols," 8A.

Leviticus 19:1-18

of all the other commandments: "you shall love your neighbor as yourself: I am the Lord" (Lev 19:18). A person who follows the commandment to love is simply not going to steal, lie, defraud, slander, hate, or bear a grudge.

This passage ends with a focus on the holiness that comes from a life of loving our neighbors as ourselves. Leviticus 19 is one of the Bible's greatest hits because it contains this verse which Jesus included in his Great Commandment (Matt 22:39), and which the apostle Paul referenced when he said, "The whole law is summed up in a single commandment, 'You shall love your neighbor as yourself'" (Gal 5:14). With love as our yardstick, we stand a good chance of being a holy people who serve a holy God.

Questions:

1. Where do you see the temptation of idolatry in your own life?
2. What are the most dangerous idols in the world around you?
3. How is love of neighbor connected to a life of holiness?

4

Numbers 21:4–9

BECAUSE IT IS FILLED with many numbers and census lists, the fourth book of the Bible is called "Numbers." Early in the first chapter, God says to Moses, "Take a census of the whole congregation of Israelites" (Num 1:2). But the Hebrew tradition calls the book *Bamidbar,* which is translated into English as "in the wilderness." The people of Israel remain in the wilderness for the length of this book, moving from Mount Sinai toward the Promised Land.

The Bible's greatest hit in the book of Numbers is a curious little story about a bronze serpent. As the people of Israel traveled around the land of Edom, they became impatient and spoke against God and Moses, saying, "Why have you brought us up out of Egypt to die in the wilderness?" (Num 21:5). Now impatience is something we all feel from time to time, whether we are stuck in traffic or waiting for someone to serve us. Usually, we become impatient when our expectations are not met. What got the Israelites in trouble was their expectation that Moses and God would give them a quick and comfortable trip to the Promised Land. When Moses and God did not conform to their expectations, they became impatient. If the Buddha had been with them on their journey, he would have told them that expectations cause suffering. The people also fell into complaining about having no food, even though they were being given manna in the wilderness. They were like the old joke about senior citizens at a resort. One says, "Boy, the food at this place is really terrible." The other says, "Yeah, and such small portions."

As a result, they were invaded by a dangerous species of "poisonous serpents" (Num 21:6). The serpents were an invasive species, similar to the

Numbers 21:4–9

creatures now coming from overseas on ships and planes and invading the United States: Asian tiger mosquitoes, Northern snakeheads, Mexican fruit flies, and brown marmorated stink bugs. These creatures are dangerous because they have no natural enemies in the US, and they do extensive damage to our landscape, vegetation, and wildlife. Their invasions are not so much the will of God as they are the result of human activity, just as the arrival of the poisonous serpents was the result of the sinfulness of the Israelites. In the year 2010, the brown marmorated stink bug took a $37 million bite out of the Mid-Atlantic's apple crop. According to *The Washington Post*, this invasive species also attacks peaches, grapes, and other fruit, and it has the nasty habit of crawling into houses and sometimes climbing into the beds of sleeping humans at night.[1]

The people of Israel needed help with their invasive species, so they confessed their sins and asked for Moses to pray that God would take away the serpents. Moses prayed, and God said, "'Make a poisonous serpent, and set it on a pole; and everyone who is bitten shall look at it and live.' So Moses made a serpent of bronze, and put it upon a pole; and whenever a serpent bit someone, that person would look at the serpent of bronze and live" (Num 21:8–9). The word "poisonous" comes from the Hebrew *seraph* and can also be translated "fiery." The same word is found in Isaiah, when a seraph flew to the prophet, holding a burning coal (Isa 6:6).

God offered an innovative solution to their problem, and it worked perfectly. Whenever snake-bitten people looked at the serpent of bronze, they survived. The power of the serpent of bronze did not come from magic, but from its ability to inspire the people to move their focus from themselves to God. Healing came from looking up at the serpent with faith and trusting its ability to connect a person to the power of God. This set a pattern for all the generations of people that followed, including us. Whenever we are bitten by sin, we can look to God and live. Sins of impatience and complaining are as real for us today as they were for the people of Israel, and when we look at the book of Numbers, we cannot help but see a portrait of ourselves.

But Numbers is also a portrait of God, and a particularly clear portrayal of God's justice and mercy. Numbers says that God sends the poisonous serpents to bite the impatient, complaining people—that's God's punishment of sin. But God also sends a means of salvation by instructing Moses to make a bronze serpent and put it on a pole—that's God's merciful

---

1. Fears, "Invasive bugs," A1.

offer of forgiveness and new life. Numbers tells us that God is responsible both for the poisonous serpents that bite the people and for the bronze serpent that saves the people.

This biblical story may seem obscure to us, but Jesus knew it well. That's why he used it to describe himself in the Gospel of John, saying, "Just as Moses lifted up the serpent in the wilderness, so must the Son of Man be lifted up, that whoever believes in him may have eternal life" (John 3:14–15). Jesus tells us that when sin bites us, all we have to do is lift our eyes. High on the cross is the Son of Man, inviting everyone who believes in him to receive forgiveness and eternal life.

Questions:

1. What makes you fall into impatience, complaining, and anger?
2. How does God help you to deal with the sins in your life?
3. When do you lift your eyes to God or to Jesus in faith, and what is the result?

5

Deuteronomy 6:1–9

DEUTERONOMY IS THE FIFTH book of the Bible, the end of the section called The Pentateuch, which simply means "five books." The Pentateuch is often called the "Five Books of Moses" or the *Torah*, a Hebrew word that means "instructions." With the wandering in the wilderness now over, these laws were delivered in the land of Moab. *Deuteronomy* comes from a Greek word meaning "second law," and it contains the set of laws which the Israelites received as they prepared to cross the Jordan River into the Promised Land.

At the beginning of Deuteronomy 6, Moses speaks of the commandments that the people are to observe in the Promised Land: "Hear therefore, O Israel, and observe them diligently, so that it may go well with you" (Deut 6:3). This begins a section in which Moses reviews God's goodness and urges the people to behave like God's chosen people, fearing God and keeping all of God's commandments so that their "days may be long" (Deut 6:2). If the people observe the commandments diligently, it will "go well" with them, and they will multiply greatly in the land that has been promised to them (Deut 6:3). Clearly, God desires to work for good in the lives of God's people. Decrees and commandments are given for our benefit, to structure our lives in life-giving ways. Just as the game of tennis would be meaningless without lines or a net, our lives would become chaotic without the ordering of God's laws. Commandments are meant to be helpful to us, not oppressive.

Then Moses says, "Hear, O Israel: The LORD is our God, the LORD alone" (Deut 6:4). Particularly important are the verses in Chapter 6 which begin with the verb "hear," in Hebrew *shema*. Hearing is critical to the life of faith, even more important than seeing, as the apostle Paul noted when he said, "faith comes from what is heard" (Rom 10:17). Israel is challenged to hear that "The LORD is our God, the LORD alone" (Deut 6:4). When "The LORD" is written in all caps, it is a code for the personal name for Israel's God: YHWH. Since this name is regarded by many Jews as being too sacred to be pronounced, the word "LORD" is said whenever YHWH appears.

The reality of life is that other powers are constantly competing for our loyalty. "As good as we might be," I wrote in a column on idolatry in *USA Today*, "we can still be seduced by counterfeit gods. In Washington, the idol of power draws politicians and their supporters away from compromise and toward ideological purity. On Wall Street, success tempts brokers and investors to value profits over people. In Hollywood, the focus on beauty creates a standard of physical perfection that is impossible for most people to achieve. And in neighborhoods across the country, children are pampered in ways that border on idolatry, leaving them with a distorted sense of their place in the world. Each of these idols can be a good thing, when handled properly. But power, success, and even children can become obsessions and lead us down dangerous and deadly paths."[1]

Next comes the commandment to love God, introduced here for the first time. The commandment to "love the LORD your God" (Deut 6:5) is a bold new approach, one that goes on to become central to both Judaism and Christianity. Jesus later referenced this verse as the first part of his Great Commandment (Mark 12:29–30). With this commandment comes the challenge of giving priority to God, much in the way that we give priority to the people we love: spouses, children, relatives, friends, close neighbors. Love is a much stronger bond and obligation than respect, duty, or affection.

Moses continues by urging the people to keep his words in their hearts, recite them to their children, and talk about them both inside and outside their homes. "Bind them as a sign on your hand," he says, "fix them as an emblem on your forehead, and write them on the doorposts of your house" (Deut 6:8–9). Moses gives the people of Israel advice about maintaining the centrality of the commandments, in particular the Ten Commandments which are presented in the previous chapter of Deuteronomy. In Jewish tradition, these instructions are taken literally in the wearing of phylacteries, small leather containers which contain biblical tests, and the nailing of a mezuzah to a doorway. God's law is to be remembered in every aspect of life.

1. Brinton, "False idols," 8A.

Deuteronomy 6:1-9

The sixth chapter of Deuteronomy, containing the "Shema," is one of the Bible's greatest hits because it commands us to make God the highest power in our lives and to love this God with all of our heart, soul, and might. It also challenges us to remember God's commandments, to teach them to our children, and to discuss them inside and outside our homes. If we live by them—in every time and place and situation—we will discover that God has ordered our lives in a truly beneficial way.

Questions:

1. What are some of the counterfeit gods that compete for your loyalty?
2. How do God's commandments structure your activities in life-giving ways?
3. In what ways do you love God and order your life around this bond?

6

Joshua 3:7–17

JOSHUA IS THE FIRST book in the section of the Protestant Bible known as the "Historical Books." Named for its main character, the book of Joshua tells of the conquest of the land of Canaan by the Israelites. By the third chapter, the people of Israel were standing on the Moab side of the Jordan River, wondering what to do. Unlike their ancestors on the edge of the Red Sea, they had no Moses to lift his hand to part the waters. The Moses generation was passing away and the Joshua generation was rising up.

But God was with the Israelites on the banks of the Jordan River, and God had just made a promise to their new leader. "I will begin to exalt you in the sight of all Israel," said the LORD to Joshua, "so that they may know that I will be with you as I was with Moses" (Josh 3:7). God also told Joshua to command the priests who were bearing the ark of the covenant, the box which contained the law of Moses and which represented the presence of God. Joshua said to them, "When you come to the edge of the waters of the Jordan, you shall stand still in the Jordan" (Josh 3:8). And then he said to the people, "Draw near and hear the words of the LORD your God" (Josh 3:9).

Begin by listening, said Joshua. Stand still and hear the words of God. Joshua instructed the people to fall into formation behind God, not to march ahead of God. This was demonstrated when the people set out from their tents and "the priests bearing the ark of the covenant were *in front of* the people" (Josh 3:14, emphasis added). The ark represented the presence and the power of "the living God," moving ahead of the people (Josh 3:10).

We are challenged to do the same today: to listen to the word of God and follow where the living God leads us. Our Lord wants to guide us in the

Joshua 3:7–17

path that is best for us, giving us words designed to maximize our health and happiness. These include the words of Moses, "remember the sabbath day, and keep it holy" (Exod 20:8); the counsel of Isaiah, "seek justice, rescue the oppressed, defend the orphan, plead for the widow" (Isa 1:17); and the command of Jesus, "love your enemies and pray for those who persecute you" (Matt 5:44). All of this is meant to help us, not to hurt us. Keeping the sabbath gives us time for rest and renewal, caring for the poor makes our community a better place, and loving our enemies breaks the cycle of violence and revenge. Even comedian Stephen Colbert, known for his sarcastic political commentary, is a deeply committed Christian who fights for the rights of migrant workers and believes that God wants us to experience justice and joy. He put a note on his computer which said, "Joy is the most infallible sign of the presence of God."[1] Begin by listening, said Joshua—draw near and hear the word of the Lord. You will be given real guidance, and maybe even joy.

After listening, we are to *move forward one small step at a time*. When the carriers of the ark had come to the Jordan River, and the feet of the priests touched the edge of the water, "the waters flowing from above stood still, rising up in a single heap" (Josh 3:16). Notice that the priests just dipped their feet into the edge of the water, instead of plunging into the deepest part of the river. They watched and waited for God to act, which happened moments later when the waters rose up in a heap. Then the "people crossed over opposite Jericho" (Josh 3:16).

Where is it that you, as an individual, are challenged to put your feet into the water and see what God will do? Perhaps you are feeling tension in a relationship with a friend or relative, and need to pick up the phone and talk. Maybe there is a coworker you distrust, but could get to know better over coffee. It could be that your neighborhood is full of isolated individuals and families, and God is leading you to pull people together through a block party. You don't have to see the whole staircase, just the first step. If you take a step toward healing and peace, God will protect you.

Finally, *keep your eyes on the future*, not the past. Joshua tells us that the priests carrying the ark of the covenant stood on dry ground in the middle of the Jordan River until all the people finished crossing the river. Then, the priests "came up from the middle of the Jordan, and the soles of the priests' feet touched dry ground, [and] the waters of the Jordan returned to their place and overflowed all its banks, as before" (Josh 4:18). As

---

1. Rowles, "20 remarkable facts," § 9.

soon as the people crossed the river, it began to flow again. The people kept moving forward, leaving the rushing river behind them.

We are challenged to look to the future as well, without beating ourselves up over the mistakes of the past. The crossing of the Jordan River is one of the Bible's greatest hits because it tells us that our security comes from the God who walks with us into the future, giving us the help we need each day. Along with the people of Israel, we are challenged to walk by faith into the Promised Land, surrounded by the presence and the power of the living God.

Questions:

1. When do you take time to stand still and listen for the voice of God?
2. How are you moving forward in faith, one small step at a time?
3. What is the value of looking to the future instead of the past?

7

Judges 4:1–10

THE SECOND OF THE Historical Books, called Judges, is named after the main characters of the book. But unlike our judges today, their work was not primarily legal. Instead, they were leaders of the tribes of Israel, and they often led the military in heroic ways. Their leadership offered stability to the tribes of Israel before the monarchy was established, during a time in which a particular pattern repeated itself: The people of Israel were unfaithful to God, they were oppressed by a foreign people, they cried out to God, and God sent judges to lead them.

This pattern is seen at the beginning of the fourth chapter, when the Israelites again did what was evil in the sight of God. "So the LORD sold them into the hand of King Jabin of Canaan, who reigned in Hazor; the commander of his army was Sisera" (Judg 4:2). The evil of the Israelites was largely the worship of the false gods of Canaan, which led to punishment from the God of Israel. Clearly, the oppression of the Israelites was not a random historical event—the Book of Judges portrays it as a punishment for their unfaithfulness, one that is delivered by King Jabin of Canaan and his general Sisera. This time of suffering lasted for twenty years, an entire generation, and "the Israelites cried out to the LORD for help" (Judg 4:3).

In response to their cries, God sent judges to the people, again and again. In the fourth chapter, the judge is Deborah, described later as "a mother in Israel" (Judg 5:7)—a strong, courageous, and independent woman. "At that time Deborah, a prophetess, wife of Lappidoth, was judging Israel. She used to sit under the palm of Deborah . . . and the Israelites came up to her for judgment" (Judg 4:4–5). Deborah was both a prophet and a judge—an early indication that God calls both women and men to leadership. Prophets were both truth-tellers and fortune-tellers in the Bible; they could see the truth about injustice in society and predict the consequences of that condition. In the twentieth century, the Rev. Dr. Martin Luther King Jr. acted like a biblical prophet in that he spoke the truth about racism in the United States and said, "I've seen the Promised Land. I may not get there with you. But I want you to know tonight, that we, as a people, will get to the Promised Land." The day after he spoke these prophetic words, King was assassinated.[1] King saw both the truth and the future, and he spoke clearly about them.

Although Deborah was a powerful judge and a prophet, she did not attempt to fight her battles alone. Judges tells us that she summoned a military man named Barak and delivered God's command to take a position at Mount Tabor, bringing ten thousand fighters. "I will draw out Sisera, the general of Jabin's army," promised God, "to meet you by the Wadi Kishon with his chariots and his troops; and I will give him into your hand" (Judg 4:7). Barak was receptive to this order, but under one condition: "If you will go with me," he said, "I will go; but if you will not go with me, I will not go" (Judg 4:8). This man of war knew that he and his men needed Deborah's support and encouragement, and he wanted her to bless the expedition and share in God's victory. This became a clear example of shared leadership, with a man and a woman both playing important roles.

Deborah agreed, since she believed as God's prophet that the battle belonged to God. But she made a prediction: "I will surely go with you; nevertheless, the road on which you are going will not lead to your glory, for the LORD will sell Sisera into the hand of a woman" (Judg 4:9). Deborah may have sensed that Barak was not quite faithful enough to enjoy victory on his own, and that glory in battle would belong to another. She predicted that victory over Sisera would come from a woman, but at this point the identity of the woman was not clear. It could be Deborah, or it could be another woman.

In verses beyond this passage, we hear the rest of the story—one in which a woman named Jael played a critical role. When Barak and Deborah led their ten thousand warriors against the Canaanites, Sisera fled from battle and was killed by Jael, who drove a tent peg into his temple while he slept in her tent (Judg 4:21). Like so many biblical characters, Jael was a complex character, not entirely good or bad. Yes, she completed the Israelite

---

1. King, "I've Been to the Mountaintop," § 1.

Judges 4:1-10

victory by killing Sisera the Canaanite general. But she did this by violating a central rule of hospitality, which called for the protection of one's guests.

This was the last of the struggles between the Israelites and the residents of Canaan, and it resulted in a period of peace that lasted forty years. After this, the fights were all between the Israelites and foreign invaders such as the Moabites, the Edomites, and the Ammonites. This story is one of the Bible's greatest hits because it shows the potential for shared leadership between men and women, and the ways in which God responds to the cries of God's people by sending strong, courageous, and insightful people to lead God's people into security and peace.

Questions:

1. Who are today's truth-telling prophets?
2. Where do you see examples of shared leadership, involving women and men?
3. How do you see God using complex characters to accomplish God's goals today?

8

Ruth 1:1–18

IN THE CHRISTIAN OLD Testament, the Book of Ruth follows the Book of Judges, probably based on its opening line, "In the days when the judges ruled . . ." (Ruth 1:1). In the Jewish scriptures, the book is found in the final section called Writings. In this time of judges, there was a famine in the land, so a man of Bethlehem went to the land of Moab, along with his wife Naomi and two sons. The man died and his two sons married a couple of Moabite women named Orpah and Ruth. But then the two sons died, leaving Naomi without a husband or sons.

So, what was poor Naomi supposed to do? She decided to return to Judah, where the famine was now over. But she knew that she had nothing to offer her daughters-in-law, so she said, "Go back each of you to your mother's house. May the LORD deal kindly with you" (Ruth 1:8). All three wept, and the daughter-in-law named Orpah departed, but Ruth clung to her mother-in-law. Naomi said to her, "See, your sister-in-law has gone back to her people and to her gods; return after your sister-in-law" (Ruth 1:15). But Ruth, determined to stay with Naomi, came up with one of the greatest lines in the Bible, "Where you go, I will go; where you lodge, I will lodge; your people shall be my people, and your God my God. Where you die, I will die—there will I be buried!" (Ruth 1:16–17). When Naomi saw that Ruth was faithful to her and determined to stay with both her and her God, Naomi allowed her to come along.

This line is a powerful statement of love and faithfulness, and it has shaped human life for centuries. Ruth's words are like the lines from a movie that remain lodged in our hearts and minds long after the film has ended. Think of *The Wizard of Oz* (1939), in which Dorothy says to her dog, "Toto, I've a feeling we're not in Kansas anymore." People quote that line whenever they feel like the world around them has changed. *Cool Hand Luke* (1967) gave us the words, "What we've got here is a failure to communicate." You'll hear that one when people suffer a complete breakdown in communication. From *This is Spinal Tap* (1984) we get the line, "These go to eleven." According to *The Washington Post*, Christopher Guest was referring to custom amps that don't max out at a measly ten. Now, turning something up to eleven can mean any type of excessiveness.[1]

The world of movies, of course, is not the only source of lines that shape our lives. The Bible is also full of great phrases: "The Lord is my shepherd, I shall not want" (Psalm 23:1); "For surely I know the plans I have for you, says the LORD" (Jer 29:11); "Love is patient; love is kind" (1 Cor 13:4–5); "I can do all things through him who strengthens me" (Phil 4:13); "all things work together for good for those who love God" (Rom 8:28). And, of course, there is the verse that Martin Luther called "the Gospel in miniature," from John: "For God so loved the world that he gave his only Son, so that everyone who believes in him may not perish but may have eternal life" (John 3:16).

What is so special about these lines from the Bible? For starters, they are true—they capture an important insight about the nature of God and human beings. But great lines also shape us because they capture an entire story. When Dorothy says, "We're not in Kansas anymore," you know that she has entered the strange new world of Oz. The line becomes a shorthand description of the entire movie. "Where you go, I will go; where you lodge, I will lodge" (Ruth 1:16) tells us something essential about Ruth, but these words also summarize the entire story of Ruth, and remind us that God used this loving and faithful woman in a powerful way. Ruth went to Bethlehem with Naomi, met a man named Boaz, married him and had a son who became the grandfather of David. Because Ruth remained faithful, she was able to become the ancestor of the greatest of Israel's kings. She did this as a Moabite woman, which sends the message that the faith of the people of Judah should be inclusive, rather than exclusive.

Although love and faithfulness cannot be seen with our eyes, they are an important reality. In the movie *A Beautiful Mind* (2001), a brilliant mathematician named John Nash suffers from terrible hallucinations. After a particularly threatening episode, his wife Alicia comes to him and asks,

---

1. Merry, "As if," § 4.

"You want to know what's real?" Putting his hand on her heart, she says, "This is real." She remains faithful to him in the face of an uncertain future, and at the end of his life he wins the Nobel Prize.

"This is real," says Alicia Nash—you are not alone. "This is real," says Ruth to Naomi—I will be with you. This is God's promise to us, as well—that nothing in all creation will separate us from our Lord. "Where you go, I will go; where you lodge, I will lodge." This promise from Ruth to Naomi is one of the Bible's greatest hits because it is God's promise to each of us. "You want to know what's real?" *This* is real—the love and faithfulness of the one true God, in every time and place, in the face of any hardship, loss, or failure. This line from the Book of Ruth is one that can truly shape our lives.

Questions:

1. What is your favorite line from Scripture, and why?
2. How is the character of God revealed to you in the Book of Ruth?
3. Where can the church be more inclusive of different cultures?

9

1 Samuel 17:32–49

THE BOOK OF SAMUEL was originally a single book, but was eventually divided into 1 Samuel and 2 Samuel. The book is named after Samuel, a judge and a prophet who anointed Saul and David as the first two kings of Israel. In chapter 17, King Saul had the Israelite army at his disposal, but he seemed powerless in the face of a giant named Goliath and the army of the Philistines. Then young David went to the battlefield, saw the giant, and asked his fellow Israelites, "Who is this uncircumcised Philistine that he should defy the armies of the living God?" (1 Sam 17:26). David puts his trust not in the skill of the Israelite army, but in the power of the "living God."

David went to Saul to volunteer his services, saying, "Let no one's heart fail because of him; your servant will go and fight with this Philistine." Saul said to David, "You are not able to go against this Philistine to fight with him; for you are just a boy" (1 Sam 17:32–33). Goliath stood a towering nine feet, six inches. He had a helmet of bronze, a coat of mail, a shield, and armor on his shins. For weapons, he carried a javelin and a spear. David, on the other hand, was a youth who had no helmet, armor, or sword. His only weapon was a sling and five stones. He was clearly the underdog, but David convinced Saul that he had vital experience as a shepherd, with a record of killing predators that threatened his sheep. David said, "The Lord, who saved me from the paw of the lion and from the paw of the bear, will save me from the hand of this Philistine." So Saul said, "Go, and may the Lord be with you!" (1 Sam 17:37).

Originally, Saul clothed David with his armor and weapons, but David removed them and picked up his staff, his shepherd's bag, his sling, and five smooth stones. When Goliath saw David, he sneered and said, "Come to me, and I will give your flesh to the birds of the air and to the wild animals of the field" (1 Sam 17:44). David accepted his invitation, running quickly toward the battle line to meet him. David took a stone from his bag and slung it hard into Goliath's forehead. Goliath fell to the ground and David cut off his head, using the giant's own sword. Score one for the underdog.

Although this seems to be a surprising victory, it actually makes perfect sense. History teaches us that Davids are usually insurgents, finding novel ways to defeat their enemies. They refuse to play by Goliath's rules, but instead adopt unconventional strategies. In *The New Yorker* magazine, Malcolm Gladwell has explained the secrets of being a successful underdog by talking about the game of basketball, in which towering Goliaths usually win by rising over their shorter opponents. But Gladwell believes that Davids can win by using the full-court press, a strategy in which you prevent your opponent from advancing up the court to the basket. If you are a David, and you allow a Goliath get to the basket, he is probably going to score. But if you press him, and keep him at the other end of the court for a significant amount of time, you stand a chance of winning.[1] When David "ran quickly toward the battle line to meet the Philistine" (1 Sam 17:48), he was an underdog using the full-court press to beat a giant.

If we want to win the daunting battles we face, we shouldn't play by Goliath's rules. Instead, we have to adopt a David strategy. We can begin by *choosing an unconventional approach*, based on our unique talents. King Saul said to David, "you are just a boy, and he has been a warrior from his youth" (1 Sam 17:33). Saul was right. David could not stand up to Goliath as a conventional warrior. But David could fight as a highly-skilled shepherd boy, with five smooth stones and a sling.

Next, *try harder than anyone else*, substituting effort for ability. David rose early in the morning to take food to the fearful Israelite soldiers. After volunteering to fight, David stood before Goliath and boldly predicted, "This very day the LORD will deliver you into my hand" (1 Sam 17:46). In doing so, David not only tried harder but he *believed* harder—he surpassed his fellow Israelites in showing confidence that God would exert effort on their behalf. David believed that "the battle is the LORD's and he will give [Goliath] into our hand" (1 Sam 17:47).

Finally, *be an insurgent*, challenging authorities about how things are supposed to be done. David was an insurgent when he "ran quickly

---

1. Gladwell, "How David Beats Goliath," § 5.

1 Samuel 17:32–49

toward the battle line" (1 Sam 17:48). He disrupted the normal rhythm of the battle, in which the Philistines stood on one mountain and Israel stood on another mountain, with periodic fighting in the valley between them. David decided to do something different, running toward Goliath with a full-court press.

The story of David and Goliath is one of the Bible's greatest hits because it shows us that we can be victorious when we choose an unconventional approach, try harder than anyone else, and challenge authority. Each of us is part of the "armies of the living God" (1 Sam 17:36), given a unique set of talents by a God who wants us to be triumphant in the battles we face.

Questions:

1. When have you been an underdog in a personal battle?
2. What God-given talents did you use?
3. When have you challenged authorities, and what was the result?

10

2 Samuel 11:1–15

DAVID IS THE KEY character in 2 Samuel, since the narrative covers events that happen after the death of the prophet Samuel. The book begins with news of King Saul's death, after which the people of the southern kingdom of Judah decide to name David as king. God promises that David's dynasty will be preserved forever, and it certainly remains in the hearts of God's people through the time of Jesus, the one whose father Joseph is "from the house and family of David" (Luke 2:4). But in spite of this promise, King David soon gets himself in trouble.

"In the spring of the year, the time when kings go out to battle, David sent Joab with his officers and all Israel with him; they ravaged the Ammonites, and besieged Rabbah. But David remained at Jerusalem" (2 Sam 11:1). David's problems began in the spring, the time each year when "kings"—that is, serious kings—"go out to battle." But instead of doing his job and leading his soldiers, David remained in the comfort and safety of Jerusalem, shirking his duties. "It happened, late one afternoon, when David rose from his couch and was walking about on the roof of the king's house, that he saw from the roof a woman bathing; the woman was very beautiful" (2 Sam 11:2). After getting up from a nap, David saw a naked woman, liked what he saw, and found out that she was "Bathsheba daughter of Eliam, the wife of Uriah the Hittite" (2 Sam 11:3). She was the daughter of Eliam, one of David's "mighty men" (2 Sam 23:34), and was also the wife of Uriah, a foreign Hittite who was nonetheless a soldier of Israel.

What is clear from this description is that Bathsheba was off limits. But David sent messengers to fetch her, and he went to bed with her. In this terrible abuse of royal power, David shifted his attitude toward the people around him. Instead of seeing them as human beings, he looked at them as objects. Bathsheba soon sent David the message that she was pregnant. Although she had been treated like an object of desire, she was clearly a vital human being, able to play a part in the miracle of conception and birth.

But King David failed to open his eyes to this truth. Instead, he continued to treat people like objects, first by ordering his captain Joab to send him Uriah the Hittite. David told Uriah to go to his house and sleep with his wife Bathsheba, so that Uriah would cover David's tracks and obscure the paternity of the child. But Uriah was a human being, not an object. He was determined to follow his conscience instead of the commands of the king, so he slept at the entrance of the king's house, not wanting to disrespect his colleagues in the field by enjoying a night with his wife. Uriah the Hittite turned out to be a righteous foreigner, similar to Ruth the Moabite. Then David, with a heart as cold as ice, wrote a letter to Joab and forced honorable Uriah to carry it to the battlefield. "Set Uriah in the forefront of the hardest fighting," David said, "and then draw back from him, so that he may be struck down and die" (2 Sam 11:15). Joab followed these orders and Uriah was killed—tossed away like an inconvenient object.

King David's treatment of Bathsheba and Uriah is a chilling warning to us. It illustrates the deadly danger of seeing people as objects. Instead of respecting Bathsheba as a woman and a wife, David sees her as a thing designed to give him pleasure. Instead of honoring Uriah as a soldier and a husband, David disposes of him as though he were a throwaway object. This story packs an emotional punch, as it shows the great harm that can be done when we treat people as objects instead of as human beings.

Fortunately, a simple formula exists to keep us on the right track: *Love people, not things; use things, not people.* How differently the story of King David would have turned out if he had loved Bathsheba and Uriah as people, instead of treating them like objects designed to satisfy his desires and advance his agenda. *Love people, not things.* This means to see everyone as a precious child of God, made in the image of God, and to respect them as daughters, wives, sons, husbands, mothers, fathers, loyal workers, faithful fellow Christians. Love them as Christ loves them, remembering the commandment of Jesus to love one another (John 13:34). Also: *Use things, not people.* Yes, use your smartphone to communicate with friends and post pictures about your life. Use your computer to write documents and shop online. But don't ever love these things so much that they draw your attention away from the flesh-and-blood human beings around you.

"This is a classic story of the arrogant misuse of power for personal whim," writes professor of Old Testament Bruce C. Birch. "It reminds us that even those most admired and most accomplished are not immune to the temptation of power."[1] It is one of the Bible's greatest hits because it teaches us to love people instead of things, and to use things instead of people. Such guidance can be a huge help to us as we face our own objects of desire.

Questions:

1. Where are people treated like objects today, and what can we do about it?
2. What does it mean to you to love people, not things?
3. How can you properly use things, not people?

---

1. Birch, "The First and Second Books of Samuel," 1288.

11

1 Kings 19:1–15

As the first book of Kings begins, Solomon becomes ruler of the united kingdom after the reign of his father David. He builds a temple, a palace, and other royal buildings. After Solomon's death, the kingdom divides into a nation called Israel in the north and another called Judah in the south. In time, Ahab becomes king of the northern kingdom, marries a Phoenician princess named Jezebel, and erects an altar to Baal. This upsets the prophet Elijah, who has remained faithful to the God of Israel. He confronts 450 of the prophets of Baal and kills them.

But when Ahab's wife Jezebel hears what Elijah had done to the prophets of Baal, she wants to kill him. As chapter 19 begins, Elijah flees by going a day's journey into the wilderness, and sits down under a solitary broom tree. Feeling stressed and depressed, he needs some time to recharge in nature, much as Jesus did when "he would withdraw to deserted places and pray" (Luke 5:16).

This kind of escape into the wilderness is growing in popularity. Called "forest bathing," it originated in Japan and is designed to calm the spirits of people who are stressed by too much technology. According to *The Washington Post*, a group of high-tech workers in Seattle recently took part in an activity called "Unplug and Recharge in Nature." After spending so much time in the information-loaded virtual world, they felt a need to reconnect with the tree-filled real world. Research is beginning to show that this kind of bathing is associated with lower stress levels and better moods, as well as an increase in self-esteem, physical fitness, memory, attention and creativity.[1]

Participants in forest bathing are asked to find a "sit spot" and rest quietly for twenty minutes, using all of their senses to become aware of the wilderness around them. And this is exactly what Elijah did when he sat down under a broom tree. When he found his "sit spot," he was feeling discouraged and depressed, and he asked that he might die. He fell asleep, and after a while an angel touched him and said, "Get up and eat." He found a cake and a jar of water, and then he ate, drank, and lay down again (1 Kgs 19:5–6). Elijah then got up and began to exercise, traveling in the strength of that food for forty days. Forty is a number often attached to a time of testing in the Bible, such as the forty days that Jesus was tempted in the desert and the forty years that the Israelites wandered in the wilderness. But it is also a time of renewal: Jesus proved himself faithful, and the people of Israel became ready to enter the Promised Land. In Elijah's case, the forty days reconnected him with God and renewed him for further prophetic work. He traveled to Horeb, the spot where God delivered the Ten Commandments to Moses.

Next, God asked Elijah what he was doing there. Elijah complained that his fellow Israelites had forsaken God's covenant, thrown down God's altars, and killed God's prophets. "I alone am left," he cried out, "and they are seeking my life, to take it away" (1 Kgs 19:10). Poor Elijah. He had taken a forty-day forest bath, but was still feeling stressed. So God encouraged Elijah to look around. Opening your eyes is so important if you want to unplug and recharge in nature. God challenged Elijah to "Go out and stand on the mountain before the Lord, for the Lord is about to pass by" (1 Kgs 19:11). And what did Elijah see? A great wind, an earthquake, a fire, and finally the "sound of sheer silence" (1 Kgs 19:11–12). The sound of sheer silence revealed God's presence, and this led to the turning point in Elijah's story. Filled with a sense of awe, Elijah stepped out of his cave. He had been recharged by resting, eating, drinking, exercising, listening, and looking around. He had been moved by the sound of silence to leave the safety of his cave. Then the command of God came to him, "Go, return on your way," and Elijah responded (1 Kgs 19:15). He set out to continue the prophetic work that God had called him to do.

Like Elijah, we need an occasional forest bath, because stress is a big part of modern life. We feel routine stress from the pressures of work,

---

1. Schulte, "How tech workers are turning," § 1.

1 Kings 19:1-15

family, neighbors, and daily tasks. We can be hit by the stress of a sudden change, such as losing a job, going through a divorce, or struggling with an illness. Fortunately, God gives us a beautiful world in which to take a healing bath. Each of us has the power to walk away from our computers and step out into the world. Each of us can turn off our smartphones and look up at the birds in the trees. Each of us can escape the noise of our workplace or school and listen for the sounds of the natural world. This passage is one of the Bible's greatest hits because it teaches us that the glory of God can be experienced in creation, and that it can fill us with new life. Like Elijah, we can escape the stress and return refreshed.

Questions:

1. What makes you feel stressed and depressed?
2. When do you spend time in nature, and what does it do for you?
3. How have you experienced God in sheer silence?

12

2 Kings 2:1–12

THE NAME ELIJAH MEANS "My God is YHWH" (the personal name of God in Judaism is YHWH), while the name Elisha means "My God is salvation." Both men are prophets in Judaism, Christianity, and Islam, and their stories are told in the first and second books of Kings. At the beginning of 2 Kings, Elijah condemned King Ahaziah of Israel for turning to a foreign god, and Elijah called down fire from heaven on the king's messengers. Then, as the second chapter begins, "The Lord was about to take Elijah up to heaven by a whirlwind" (2 Kgs 2:1). Yes, a whirlwind. This departure was an extraordinary end to an extraordinary prophetic career. But was it really an end?

Christians believe that Elijah went to heaven in a whirlwind and later returned to earth in the Transfiguration. At that point, he appeared alongside Moses and had a conversation with Jesus, showing the disciples that Jesus was the continuation of what God had started with the Old Testament law and prophets (Mark 9:2–9). Because of his unique status, Elijah is a living link between earth and heaven—our world and God's world. He shows us that heaven is not just "the afterlife," but is a place that has an ongoing impact on the choices we make in this life. Following the example of Elijah, we can put effort into changing the world as it is into the world as it should be, remembering that Jesus taught us to pray, "Your kingdom come. Your will be done, on earth as it is in heaven" (Matt 6:10). Flying with Elijah in the whirlwind, our challenge is to do whatever we can to get the ways of the world in line with the values of heaven.

In 2 Kings 2, Elijah and his protégé Elisha traveled from Gilgal to the Jordan River. The two undoubtedly remembered their ancestors on the

2 Kings 2:1–12

banks of the river (Joshua) and on the shore of the Red Sea (Exodus), two other examples of the Bible's greatest hits. Now, in 2 Kings, "Elijah took his mantle and rolled it up, and struck the water; the water was parted to the one side and to the other, until the two of them crossed on dry ground" (2 Kgs 2:8). In all of these cases, water is a sign of the chaos that can destroy the people of God, but in every situation, God gives them safe passage. Elisha then asked his master Elijah, "Please let me inherit a double share of your spirit" (2 Kgs 2:9). Elisha wanted the spirit of his master to fill him, so that he could continue his work in the world. He wanted to pick up Elijah's mantle—the cloak that was a symbol of his authority and power—and continue his prophetic ministry.

What would it mean for us to inherit Elijah's spirit and pick up his mantle today? We can begin by listening to the prophetic words that are always a clear and constant cry for justice: "seek justice" (Isaiah 1:17), "hold fast to love and justice" (Hosea 12:6), "let justice roll down like waters" (Amos 5:24), and "do justice" (Micah 6:8). When we pick up Elijah's mantle, we take action to make sure that all of our neighbors are treated fairly, and that the weak and the poor get the help they need. Elijah himself became famous for helping a poor widow and her son, who were not only needy, but were foreigners—residents of Zarephath (1 Kgs 17). Jesus later got in trouble with his neighbors in Nazareth when he reminded them that Elijah was sent to this widow at Zarephath (Luke 4:25–26). When we inherit a double share of Elijah's spirit, we join God's prophets in seeking justice, rescuing the oppressed, and defending the rights of the poor.

As Christians, our challenge is to bring the values of heaven down to earth, and to see everyone as a part of God's valuable creation. In Dawson, Minnesota, a pastor-in-training named Mandy France had been horrified by some of the things that she had heard people saying about Islam in her prayer group at Grace Lutheran Church. So she asked her Muslim doctor, Ayaz Virji, if he would be willing to give a talk about Islam to the community. According to *The Washington Post*, about four hundred people gathered in the high school auditorium, some of whom had been critical of the talk. He addressed their concern right away by saying, "I heard many people were protesting this talk. And I have to say, that stings a little bit. I mean, do I look that intimidating? . . . Do I look like a terrorist?" He laughed, and a few people in the audience laughed as well. Then he talked for an hour about what 99.99 percent of Muslims believe—none of which has anything to do with terrorism.[1]

Pastor Mandy was following Jesus when she invited Ayaz Virji to speak. Like Jesus, she was willing to reach out to someone who was considered an outcast, and build a relationship with him. Her actions helped Dr. Virji to educate his community about Islam, a faith that considers Elijah, Elisha, and Jesus to be prophets. This passage is one of the Bible's greatest hits because it moves us from earth to heaven and from heaven to earth. That's the ride we take when we join Elijah in the whirlwind. That's what happens when we keep body and spirit together, and take actions to put the ways of the world in line with the values of heaven.

Questions:

1. How do you try to keep heaven and earth together?
2. Where do you hear prophetic calls for justice today?
3. What could it mean for us to inherit Elijah's spirit and take action in the world?

---

1. McCrummen, "Love Thy Neighbor?" § 1.

13

1 Chronicles 4:1–10

THE FIRST AND SECOND books of Chronicles were originally one, and they form the last book in the Jewish Bible. The material in 1 Chronicles includes stories from Genesis through 2 Samuel, and the first nine chapters offer the most extended genealogy in the whole Bible. Genealogy is a way to establish a connection with the past, which was as important to the Israelites as it is to us today, as we take DNA ancestry tests or use the Internet to research our family history. Throughout time, people have hungered to have a deeper understanding of themselves and their family tree.

As chapter 4 begins, we encounter the genealogy that begins with the descendants of Judah and includes "the sons of Helah: Zereth, Izhar, and Ethnan. Koz became the father of Anub, Zobebah, and the families of Aharhel son of Harum. Jabez was honored more than his brothers; and his mother named him Jabez," saying, "Because I bore him in pain" (1 Chr 4:7–9). The name Jabez means "he makes sorrowful." This is followed by the most famous verse in the book, one that has come to be called "The Prayer of Jabez." In the year 2000, an entire book was written on this verse, one that sold more than ten million copies. The verse says, "Jabez called on the God of Israel, saying, 'Oh that you would bless me and enlarge my border, and that your hand might be with me, and that you would keep me from hurt and harm!' And God granted what he asked" (1 Chr 4:10).

So, what do we know about Jabez? He was "honored more than his brothers"—in Eugene Peterson's translation of the Bible called *The Message*, "Jabez was a better man than his brothers, a man of honor."[1] Jabez

---

1. Peterson, *The Message*, 664.

called on the God of Israel, believing that the LORD was the one true God. Then he asked God to bless him, believing that blessings come from God alone. Jabez requested that God "enlarge his border," which could mean physical property or spiritual territory. He asked for God's hand to be with him, to provide for him and guide him. Finally, he prayed for God to keep him from hurt and harm, similar to the way that we ask God, in the Lord's Prayer, "deliver us from evil." First Chronicles tells us that "God granted what he asked."

This prayer seems to be quite unexceptional. But Bruce Wilkinson, the author of *The Prayer of Jabez*, writes, "I want to introduce you to the amazing truths in Jabez's prayer for blessing and prepare you to expect God's astounding answers to it *as a regular part of your life experience*. [The] Jabez prayer distills God's powerful will for your future ... it reveals that your Father longs to give you so much more than you may have ever thought to ask for."[2] Wilkinson points out four principles in this prayer. First, God wants us to pray for his blessing. Second, God wants us to pray for his blessing on our ministry to people. Third, God wants us to pray for spiritual power in our ministry efforts. Fourth, we should pray to be delivered from evil. None of these principles is unique to the prayer of Jabez, and each is taught elsewhere in the Bible. But the prayer, writes Baptist pastor Greg Gilbert, is presented "as some kind of magic formula that will somehow hypnotize God into blessing us. [Wilkinson] writes as if he has unearthed some long lost secret amulet from the caves of the Old Testament that will unlock God's vault of blessing for us."[3]

Wilkinson says that he prays the Jabez prayer "word for word," and he tells stories of people who have seen changes in their lives after "praying the prayer" for years.[4] Such an approach seems to be counter to the advice of Jesus, "When you are praying, do not heap up empty phrases ... Your Father knows what you need before you ask him" (Matt 6:7–8). Even worse, says Greg Gilbert, the message of the book is that the Jabez prayer *cannot fail* to get results. "Dear Reader," says the Preface, "I want to teach you to pray a daring prayer that God always answers." Wilkinson believes that the prayer of Jabez is a prayer that God *always* answers. "What a ridiculous and unbiblical sentence!" says Gilbert. "Christians need to recover the idea that

---

2. Wilkinson, *The Prayer of Jabez*, 11–12.
3. Gilbert, "Book Review, § 1.
4. Wilkinson, 11, 16.

1 Chronicles 4:1-10

faith is not defined as believing that God will give us what we want if we just believe hard enough."[5]

The Prayer of Jabez has been linked to the movement called "the prosperity gospel," which assumes that financial blessing is always the will of God for people of true faith. Some criticize the prayer for suggesting that God should do what people want, while traditional Christian prayer is designed to help people follow God's will. Others have criticized the book because of the way that it has been commercialized, with merchandise including key chains, mugs, backpacks, Christmas ornaments, scented candles, mouse pads, and a line of jewelry. Whether you love it or hate it, the prayer of Jabez in 1 Chronicles 4:10 is one of the Bible's greatest hits, because of the way that it inspires discussion about the power of prayer, and debate about the ways that prayer can connect people to the will of God.

Questions:

1. What is the significance of your genealogy to you?
2. When you pray for God to help you, what happens?
3. How do you pray for God's will to be done in your life?

---

[5]. Gilbert, § 1.

14

2 Chronicles 36:15–23

NEITHER OF THE BOOKS of Chronicles appears frequently in sermons and Bible studies, largely because the books repeat stories found elsewhere. Much of the material in 2 Chronicles is a repetition of the stories told in 1 and 2 Kings, with a concentration on the southern kingdom of Judah. But they have a unique and important perspective. God "had compassion on his people and on his dwelling place," says the writer of 2 Chronicles; "but they kept mocking the messengers of God, despising his words, and scoffing at his prophets, until the wrath of the LORD against his people became so great that there was no remedy" (2 Chr 36:15–16). Although God loved the Israelites and the temple, God's judgment came down on the people because of their unfaithfulness.

God took action in a surprising way, using a foreign king to advance the divine plan. According to 2 Chronicles, God "brought up against them the king of the Chaldeans, who killed their youths with the sword in the house of their sanctuary, and had no compassion on young man or young woman, the aged or the feeble; he gave them all into his hand" (2 Chr 36:17). The prophets Jeremiah and Ezekiel had spoken of the defiling of the temple by the Israelites, and now 2 Chronicles reports on the results: The Chaldeans "burned the house of God, broke down the wall of Jerusalem, burned all its palaces with fire, and destroyed all its precious vessels" (2 Chr 36:19).

Then came the exile. The king of the Chaldeans took the people of Judah into exile and made them his servants. This was done "to fulfill the word of the LORD by the mouth of Jeremiah, until the land had made up for its sabbaths. All the days that it lay desolate it kept sabbath, to fulfill seventy years" (2 Chr 36:21). Although the time of exile was full of pain and grief, it became a kind of a sabbath. In this period of sabbath rest, the land and its people became restored and ready for their next chapter. In time, "the Lord stirred up the spirit of King Cyrus of Persia," and Cyrus sent the edict: "The Lord, the God of heaven, has given me all the kingdoms of the earth, and he has charged me to build him a house at Jerusalem, which is in Judah. Whoever is among you of all his people . . . Let him go up" (2 Chr 36:22–23). The foreign king Cyrus became the "messiah" (Isa 45:1) of the Jewish people.

The writer of 2 Chronicles knows that God is the supreme ruler, master of the universe, and the one who wields ultimate power. God works the divine purposes out, both inside and outside of Israel. In this case, God moved a foreign empire on behalf of God's chosen people, and even this foreign king acknowledges that the God of Israel is "God of heaven" and the one who has given him "all the kingdoms of the earth" (2 Chr 36:23). In Christian theology, we refer to this as "the sovereignty of God."

God's sovereignty is easy to celebrate in good times, but it can be acknowledged in painful times as well. Historian Eric Washington of Calvin College has studied African American church history and discovered that many slaves found comfort in God's sovereignty, even while in captivity. "Believing in God's sovereignty gave slaves a way to see their suffering as redemptive suffering. They chose to see their suffering not in vain but as having a purpose in God's sovereign plan . . . They learned to trust in Christ through suffering. They rejoiced in Christ as they left slavery, whether through escaping, buying or being granted freedom, or emancipation."[1] From songs and spirituals that came out of the pain of slavery, it is clear that many people saw evidence of God at work throughout the journey from enslavement to freedom.

In the biblical story, God's sovereignty was revealed first in Genesis, when God said to Abraham, "I am God Almighty; walk before me, and be blameless. And I will make my covenant between me and you, and will make you exceedingly numerous" (Gen 17:1–2). God's covenant was an "everlasting covenant" (Gen 17:7) which was good news for Abraham, and is for us as well. God's covenant is everlasting because God is sovereign—able to do exactly what God wants to do, in every time, place, and situation. Abraham did not succeed in being blameless in his actions, nor did the people of Judah in the time of Jeremiah. But God Almighty proved to be the

---

1. Huyser-Honig, "Eric Washington," § 2.

God of second chances, giving people the opportunity to turn from their errors and renew their covenant with God.

We can be thankful that God always takes the lead in this relationship. This was true for Abraham and also for the Israelites in exile when, out of nowhere, "the Lord stirred up the spirit of King Cyrus of Persia" (2 Chr 36:22). The Book of 2 Chronicles reminds us that God is always faithful, even when we are not. God never breaks God's faithful and loving relationship with us, even though we often fall into faithlessness. This story is one of the Bible's greatest hits because it affirms that our promise-based relationship with God is stronger than any human failings. Our Almighty and Sovereign God can work in unexpected ways—even through King Cyrus of Persia—to save and restore God's covenant people.

Questions:

1. Where have you seen God taking action in surprising ways?
2. What does the sovereignty of God mean to you?
3. How has God been faithful to you, even in bad times?

15

Ezra 3:1–13

THE BOOK OF EZRA is named after the main character in this volume, a man who was a scribe and a priest. Overall, the book argues for national purity and exclusiveness, with a denunciation of marriages between Israelites and other tribes, a perspective that is at odds with the more inclusive message of the Book of Ruth. Ezra says that "the LORD stirred up the spirit of King Cyrus of Persia" so that he declared: "The LORD, the God of heaven, has given me all the kingdoms of the earth, and he has charged me to build him a house at Jerusalem in Judah. Any of those among you who are of his people—may their God be with them!—are now permitted to go up to Jerusalem in Judah, and rebuild the house of the LORD, the God of Israel" (Ezra 1:1–3).

When the people returned from exile, a priest named Jeshua and a governor named Zerubbabel "set out to build the altar of the God of Israel, to offer burnt offerings on it, as prescribed in the law of Moses the man of God. They set up the altar on its foundation, because they were in dread of the neighboring peoples, and they offered burnt offerings upon it to the LORD" (Ezra 3:2–3). The setting up of the altar was an act of restoration, an act that showed that Israel's religious rituals and sacrifices would be resumed in the life of the community "as prescribed in the law of Moses" (Ezra 3:2).

"Worship is the center of any thriving community of believers," writes Old Testament professor Ralph W. Klein. "The community set up the altar on its old foundations, and in the foundation deposit ceremony they probably brought a stone from the old Temple and deposited it in the new one.

Worship must be a blend of innovation and tradition."[1] At Fairfax Presbyterian Church in Virginia, where I serve as pastor, the congregation's mission statement includes the lines, "By the power of the Holy Spirit, we at FPC worship God with honesty, joy, and imagination; nourish our lives of faith in Christ; extend hospitality and grace to all people; serve a world in need; and work for reconciliation among people of diverse perspectives."

Notice that worship comes first. This priority is based on the fact that worship is what the church does most often, gathering to praise God, pray, and hear God's word every Sunday. But it also comes first because worship is the source of every other aspect of the church's life. It is only after encountering God in a service of worship that the members of the church can nourish their lives of faith in Christ, extend hospitality to all people, serve a world in need, and work for reconciliation. This priority reflects the view of the Protestant Reformer John Calvin. For him, worship was the key meeting place for God and God's people. "Wherever the faithful," he wrote, "are assembled together to engage in the solemn acts of religious worship, he is graciously present, and presides in the midst of them."[2] Worship is where we experience God's presence most frequently and powerfully, whether we are in ancient Jerusalem or in modern America.

After the establishment of the altar came the laying of the temple foundation (Ezra 3:8–13), which was followed by responsive singing: "For he is good, for his steadfast love endures forever toward Israel" (Ezra 3:11). This was the same song sung at the dedication of Solomon's temple (2 Chr 5:13). The laying of the temple foundation was a time to restore traditional worship practices, and Ezra says that when the builders laid the foundation of the temple, the priests and the Levites sang responsively, "giving thanks to the Lord, 'For he is good, for his steadfast love endures forever toward Israel.' And all the people responded with a great shout when they praised the Lord, because the foundation of the house of the Lord was laid" (Ezra 3:10–11).

But here, unlike the scene at the dedication of Solomon's temple, the sounds of praise were mixed with weeping from those who had seen the temple in its former glory. At this point in Israelite history, a moment of joy was also a moment of grief. Ezra says that "old people who had seen the first house on its foundations, wept with a loud voice when they saw this house, though many shouted aloud for joy, so that the people could

---

1. Klein, "The Books of Ezra and Nehemiah," 693.
2. Calvin, *Commentary on the Book of Psalms*, 122.

not distinguish the sound of the joyful shout from the sound of the people's weeping, for the people shouted so loudly that the sound was heard far away" (Ezra 3:12–13).

This passage from Ezra is one of the Bible's greatest hits because it reminds us that worship is central to the life of the community of faith, in ancient times and today. Worship is where we experience God's presence most frequently and powerfully, and it deserves to be a regular part of our life together. But our prayers, our praises, and our hearing of God's word does not bring a guarantee of joy. In fact, shouts of joy can be mixed with cries of grief, and a service of worship can be a complicated event. Worshipers may become upset in the course of a service, but fortunately the words from Ezra's day remain true: God "is good, for his steadfast love endures forever" (Ezra 3:11).

Questions:

1. Where is there tension between exclusiveness and inclusiveness in the church?
2. Should worship come first in the life of the church? Why or why not?
3. Where do you see joy and grief, tradition and innovation, in a service of worship?

16

Nehemiah 8:1–10

THE BOOK OF NEHEMIAH tells the story of the people of Judah, back in Jerusalem after their exile in Babylon. Their governor Nehemiah led them in rebuilding the walls of Jerusalem and instituting social and religious reforms, and the priest Ezra stood and read from Scripture while the people listened. The Word of God mattered to the people of Israel, which is why they all gathered together and "Ezra brought the law before the assembly, both men and women and all who could hear with understanding" (Neh 8:2).

Words are important in other cultures and religions as well, and sometimes people fight over them. Language riots in Algeria resulted in the deaths of people protesting the government's decision to make Arabic the official language. In Pakistan, riots led to the deaths of people protesting Urdu as the official language. Even in the United States, we have a long tradition of language battles. Ben Franklin disputed with Pennsylvania Germans in the 1750s, and more recently, language wars have pitted English-only advocates against the speakers of indigenous or immigrant languages.

A few years ago, Microsoft began to develop software to help defuse language tensions in Greece. They created software for ancient polytonic Greek—an alphabet that dates from the age of Plato. The challenge of polytonic Greek is that it has six accent marks, a much more complicated form of writing than modern monotonic Greek, which has just one accent mark. But despite the fact that it hasn't been spoken as a language for centuries, people are passionate about Plato's Greek and have gone to court over its usage. So, wanting to glide gracefully into Greek culture, Microsoft saw that it would be politically correct to offer polytonic software to the people.

Greeks love it—especially the Orthodox Church. "Ancient Greek," said one person, "is like your grandmother. You don't see her every day but you love her to death."[1]

The people of Jerusalem felt the same way about the Hebrew Scriptures, so they told Ezra to read the law of Moses, which the LORD had given to Israel. "He read from it facing the square before the Water Gate from early morning until midday, in the presence of the men and the women and those who could understand; and the ears of all the people were attentive to the book of the law" (Neh 8:3). Like Plato's Greek, the words of Moses had been missing in action, and now they were being read in the presence of the people. Ezra stood on a wooden platform and read the law, and the reading turned into a worship service that lasted about six hours. "Ezra opened the book in the sight of all the people, for he was standing above all the people; and when he opened it, all the people stood up . . . Then they bowed their heads and worshiped the LORD" (Neh 8:5–6).

The people hung on his every word, and the Hebrew text was interpreted by leaders standing nearby. You see, even though Ezra was reading the Scriptures loud and clear, the people could not understand them completely until they were interpreted in the more familiar Aramaic. Like worshipers today, they needed Scripture to be read and interpreted. A group of leaders "helped the people to understand the law, while the people remained in their places. So they read from the book, from the law of God, with interpretation. They gave the sense, so that the people understood the reading. And Nehemiah, who was the governor, and Ezra the priest and scribe, and the Levites who taught the people said to all the people, 'This day is holy to the LORD your God; do not mourn or weep.' For all the people wept when they heard the words of the law" (Neh 8:7–9). When they grasped what they were hearing, they were so moved that they cried. What is remarkable about this passage is the power of the Word of God to penetrate the human spirit, to speak to the heart, to touch the deepest corners of the soul.

The people of Jerusalem gathered beneath a wooden platform and listened to the law of God being read. They knew that to "understand" the Bible means, quite literally, to "stand under" the Bible—to place ourselves under its authority, to take it personally, to allow our lives to be shaped by it and to give it our trust and our confidence. When we seek to understand the Bible, we are doing more than making an effort to understand what

---

1. Delaney, "Plato's Greek," B1.

the words mean. Instead, we are "standing under" Scripture's view of God and humanity and sacred history, and giving it not only the insight of our brains, but also the allegiance of our hearts.

Then Nehemiah told them to go off and celebrate, because "the joy of the Lord is your strength" (Neh 8:10). This passage is one of the Bible's greatest hits because it reminds us of the power of the Word of God to refresh our souls and guide our steps. Like the people of Jerusalem, we understand Scripture best when we "stand under" God's Word and allow it to shape our hearts, souls, and minds. When the Word is read and interpreted, we share the experience of the Israelites, who wept and rejoiced "because they had understood the words that were declared to them" (Neh 8:12).

Questions:

1. What type of words are most important to you, and why?
2. How does interpretation enhance your understanding of the Bible?
3. What does it mean to you to "stand under" Scripture?

17

Esther 7:1–10

IN THE PROTESTANT BIBLE, Esther is the last of the Historical Books. It is named after a Jewish woman, Esther, who was made queen of Persia by King Ahasuerus. Her rise to prominence began when Esther won the favor of a eunuch and was brought to the king, who fell in love with her. But the situation became complicated when Esther's cousin Mordecai refused to bow down before Haman, a high official in the king's court. After Haman learned that Mordecai was a Jew, he devised a plan to kill all the Jews in the kingdom. The Book of Esther teaches us that God is at work to deliver us from destruction, provided we wisely and courageously engage the world around us.

When Mordecai learned of the plot to kill the Jews, he told Esther and she decided to take action. At the start, Esther had no clear vision of how she could save her people, since she and her cousin were aliens in a strange land—Jews living in the Persian Empire in the fifth century before Christ. But they did not let their outsider status prevent them from engaging the great powers of the empire. They developed a set of standards that would be called "Rules of Engagement" today. The FBI has these rules, as does the U.S. military and NATO. Rules of Engagement are ground rules for responding to threats and intimidation. They're specific procedures that provide guidance on when and how to employ force against an enemy.[1] Esther and Mordecai developed a set of rules that ensured that Haman, the architect of the anti-Semitic plot, would be neutralized.

---

1. Kingsley, "What are 'Rules of Engagement'?" § 2.

Esther and Mordecai were not perfect people, but they performed well in a complex and confusing situation. Intrigue, deceit, and hatred run throughout the Book of Esther, whether the spotlight is on the Jews or their enemies. And yet, this book is accepted as sacred Scripture, and is a reminder that God is at work in situations marked by anger and aggression, in places where laws are ignored and the name of God is never mentioned. In short, our LORD is active in the real world—the down-and-dirty world of politics and power-plays.

So what were the Rules of Engagement that Esther and Mordecai used as they engaged the powers of the Persian Empire? The first was: *Act*. Although she was putting herself in danger by acting, Esther arrived at the court of the king "for just such a time as this" (Esther 4:14). Choosing inaction would be suicide, both for Esther and for the Jews of Persia. At a royal feast Queen Esther said to the king, "If I have won your favor, O king, and if it pleases the king, let my life be given me—that is my petition—and the lives of my people—that is my request. For we have been sold, I and my people, to be destroyed, to be killed, and to be annihilated" (Esther 7:3–4). At the right time, she took bold action to save the lives of herself and her people.

Then she moved to the second Rule of Engagement: *Collaborate*. Esther and Mordecai knew that everyone had to be on the same page and acting in concert. Esther instructed Mordecai to gather the Jews for a fast (Esther 4:16) and then said to the king, "If we had been sold merely as slaves, men and women, I would have held my peace; but no enemy can compensate for this damage to the king" (Esther 7:4). She stated her case in such a way that she showed that she was concerned not only for her fellow Jews but for the king himself. Then the king asked her, "Who is he, and where is he, who has presumed to do this?" Esther said, "A foe and enemy, this wicked Haman!" The book says that "Haman was terrified before the king and the queen" (Esther 7:5–6).

Although Esther had identified the evildoer, she was not yet out of danger. The king left the feast in anger and went into the palace garden, but Haman stayed behind to beg that Queen Esther spare his life. Esther was in danger by staying alone with Haman, but it was a risk that she was willing to take, in order to achieve her goals. The third Rule of Engagement, *Risk*, was an important part of her plan, and her risk paid off beautifully. The book reports that one of the eunuchs said, "'Look, the very gallows that Haman has prepared for Mordecai, whose word saved the king, stands at Haman's house, fifty cubits high.' And the king said, 'Hang him on that.'

Esther 7:1-10

So they hanged Haman on the gallows that he had prepared for Mordecai" (Esther 7:9-10).

Act. Collaborate. Risk. Although Christians will take a variety of approaches to political action, the God of Esther demands some kind of engagement with the world around us. After all, we follow a Christ who calls us not to disengage, but to engage—to go into the world "like sheep into the midst of wolves . . . wise as serpents and innocent as doves" (Matt 10:16). This passage from Esther is one of the Bible's greatest hits because it challenges us to engage the world that God loves so much, and to develop rules that will enable us to act, to collaborate, and to take risks, based on our deepest religious commitments.

Questions:

1. When have you taken bold action, and what was the result?
2. Where do you see value in collaboration with people around you?
3. What kinds of risks are you willing to take, based on your faith?

18

Job 38:1–7

JOB IS THE FIRST of five poetic books, the beginning of a new section of the Bible that includes Psalms, Proverbs, Ecclesiastes, and the Song of Songs. The Book of Job is the story of a blameless and upright man who experienced the loss of his property, his children, and his health, throwing him into a profound personal crisis. Although Job had lived a righteous life, he suffered for no apparent reason, and the book raises the question of why really bad things happen to truly good people. His wife responded to his situation by saying to him, "Do you still persist in your integrity? Curse God, and die" (Job 2:9). A group of friends accused Job of wrongdoing, and suggested that his suffering was a punishment for sin. Then God shifted Job's perspective by inviting him into deep reflection about who he was in relation to God, without giving quick or easy answers.

We need to do this kind of deep work, now more than ever. In the world today, our electronic devices are constantly calling out to us, but research is revealing that we should make an effort to avoid distractions. In his *Hidden Brain* podcast, Shankar Vedantam profiles Cal Newport, a computer scientist and author of a book called *Deep Work: Rules for Focused Success in a Distracted World*. Newport says that when we let text messages, phone calls, emails, or Facebook messages guide our workday, we're weakening our ability to do the most challenging kind of work: "deep work." This is the work that requires sustained attention, such as writing a report, solving an engineering problem, or doing significant research. The solution to distractions, according to Newport, is to set aside long portions of many days to focus on deeper thinking. This means no social media, limited email, and strict limits on appointments. The result is a life that is richer and more human than a life of robotically responding to emails and messages.[1]

In chapter 38, God challenges Job to do the "deep work" *of answering the question of who he is in relation to God.* "Where were you when I laid the foundation of the earth?" asked God (Job 38:4). In other words, "Where were *you*—Job—when *I*—God—laid the foundation of the earth?" Both the "you" and the "I" are important here. In his book *Institutes of the Christian Religion,* Protestant reformer John Calvin wrote, "Our wisdom, in so far as it ought to be deemed true and solid Wisdom, consists almost entirely of two parts: the knowledge of God and of ourselves." Knowledge of God and knowledge of ourselves are interrelated, and we cannot have one without the other. "As these are connected together by many ties," says Calvin, "it is not easy to determine which of the two precedes and gives birth to the other."[2]

That's why God asks Job from the whirlwind, "Where were you when I laid the foundation of the earth? Tell me, if you have understanding" (Job 38:4). Knowledge of both God and self are important. "Who determined its measurements?" God asks. "[Who] laid its cornerstone when the morning stars sang together and all the heavenly beings shouted for joy?" (Job 38:5–7). Writing in the journal *Interpretation,* pastor Tom Are points out that "the voice in the whirlwind asks a series of questions that Job cannot answer." Job does not know the answers because he is finite. Only the infinite God knows. "This is perhaps the first word from the whirlwind: Job is creature, not creator."[3] The deep question "Who is God?" can best be answered with the word "Creator."

But since knowledge of God is connected to knowledge of self, we are also challenged to go deep into the question, "Who are *we*?" What does it mean to be human creatures? God answers this, in part, as the one "who has put wisdom in the inward parts" and "given understanding to the mind" (Job 38:36). As creatures made in the image of God, we are people who are given wisdom and understanding by our Creator. We do not have all the answers—only God does. But we do have the ability to search for answers as we live in relationship with God and with one another. "The world is complex and painful," writes Are. "But the [God] who laid the foundations of the world did so in order that there might be a world, and so that we

---

1. Vedantam, "The value of 'Deep Work,'" § 1.
2. Calvin, *Institutes of the Christian Religion,* § 1.
3. Are, "Job 38:1–7," 295.

might be in it."[4] Our Creator wants to live in relationship with us, and to share wisdom, understanding, and love with us.

When we go deep for answers, we discover that our Creator is the source of all wisdom and understanding. Calvin knew this, saying that "the endowments which we possess cannot possibly be from ourselves; nay, that our very being is nothing else than subsistence in God alone."[5] This passage from Job is one of the Bible's greatest hits because it challenges us to search for knowledge of God as Creator and knowledge of ourselves as creatures. When we put the two together, we are doing the deep work that God wants us to do.

Questions:

1. What kinds of daily distractions keep you from doing "deep work"?
2. Where do you see a link between knowledge of God and knowledge of self?
3. Which qualities shared by Creator and creature are most important to you?

---

4. Are, 298.
5. Calvin, § 1.

19

Psalm 23

THE HEBREW TITLE FOR this book is *Tehillim*, which is translated as "praises." Together, this collection of praise songs served as the hymnbook of the people of Israel. "The Book of Psalms has no plot to summarize, no narrative to recall," writes professor of Old Testament Tyler Mayfield. "It is a collection of 150 prayers and songs that give praise to God, Zion, and the king; give thanks to God and ask God for deliverance; announce trust in God; and petition God."[1]

Although these songs and prayers have great breadth, they also have depth. The most famous is Psalm 23, which describes God as a shepherd who cares for us in every time and place and situation. This God is eternally faithful to us, surrounding us with steadfast love both in life and in death. From a geometric point of view, you could say that the God of Psalm 23 is a circle, encompassing all of life with perfect symmetry. And while this might seem like an odd description of God, it connects nicely with the structure of the universe. A Nobel Prize-winning physicist named Frank Wilczek says that "the world is a piece of art," distinctive for "the outstanding role of symmetry." He points to a shape found throughout the universe—the circle—which is symmetrical because "you can rotate it around its center and it will remain a circle." In physics and mathematics, the *principle of symmetry can be described as "change without change."*[2]

The shepherd of Psalm 23 is, like the circle, an example of "change without change." God is symmetrical in the sense that God is the same from

---

1. Mayfield, *A Guide to Bible Basics*, 115.
2. Grolle, "Nobel Physicist Frank Wilczek," § 1.

any angle: A shepherd who "makes me lie down in green pastures ... leads me beside still waters ... restores my soul ... leads me in right paths". . . and then a host who prepares "a table" and anoints "my head with oil" (Psalm 23:2–5). What is true for the circle is also true for God; the circle rotates, but still remains a circle. God is active as a protective shepherd and as a gracious host, but still remains God. Change without change.

Psalm 23 is also a circle that turns through a number of daily activities. This is "a psalm about living," says biblical scholar J. Clinton McCann, Jr., "for it puts daily activities, such as eating, drinking and seeking security, in a radically God-centered perspective."[3] The psalm takes us through the circle of life, and it challenges us to put God at the center. "The Lord is my shepherd," says the psalm, "I shall not want." In the ancient world, kings were supposed to be the shepherds of their people, and in the circle of Psalm 23, God is portrayed as the greatest of shepherds, providing food in "green pastures," drink from "still waters," and guidance in "right paths" (Psalm 23:2–3).

The circle keeps turning, from food to drink to physical safety, and, in all of these areas, God gives us everything we need. Through all of the changes of life, God consistently provides for us, even in the most challenging and stressful of circumstances—serious illness, betrayal by a friend, marital problems, the loss of a job, or the death of a loved one. "Even though I walk through the darkest valley," says the psalm, "I fear no evil; for you are with me; your rod and your staff—they comfort me" (Psalm 23:4). Bible scholar McCann says that this verse is "the structural and theological center of Psalm 23," reminding us that even in "the most life-threatening situation, God's provision is sufficient." This verse describes the character of the shepherd who is at the center of the circle. Everything else revolves around it.

As the circle of the psalm continues to turn, God transitions from a caring shepherd to a gracious host. Once again, God's goodness remains constant while the situation changes. "You prepare a table before me in the presence of my enemies," says the writer of the psalm; "you anoint my head with oil; my cup overflows" (Psalm 23:5). In this section, the host does exactly what the shepherd did at the beginning of the psalm—provides food, drink, and protection. Change without change.

Through all of the difficult and disturbing changes of life, we are cared for by a changeless God. Although we face threats to our physical, emotional, and spiritual health, we have a God at the center of our lives who

3. McCann, "The Book of Psalms," 767–71.

gives us the assurance that "surely goodness and mercy shall follow me all the days of my life, and I shall dwell in the house of the Lord my whole life long" (Psalm 23:6). God offers us a symmetrical life—one in which today's threats are balanced by God's help, today's needs are balanced by God's gifts, and tomorrow's uncertainties are balanced by God's promises. Psalm 23 is one of the Bible's greatest hits because it reveals to us that God is eternally faithful to us, change without change, and that God is constantly at work in our lives, giving us everything we need.

Questions:

1. How have you experienced God as a shepherd and a host?
2. In a changing world, what does it mean to say God is changeless?
3. What is the value of having God at the center of your life?

20

Proverbs 8:1–31

THE QUESTION OF HOW to live a good life is at the heart of the Book of Proverbs, a collection of pithy sayings. The book begins with words about wisdom and knowledge, and the eighth chapter describes wisdom as a woman, a female figure who takes her stand in the middle of society and cries out, "To you, O people, I call, and my cry is to all that live" (Prov 8:4). Wisdom offers her insights to everyone who is willing to listen, and she promises wonderful gifts to anyone who will embrace her—gifts of intelligence, truth, instruction, knowledge, justice, righteousness, and wealth.

Wisdom doesn't give her gifts only to undergrads at Harvard, or techno-geeks at Microsoft, or think-tankers in the Nation's Capital. Her cry "is to all that live" (Prov 8:4). Wisdom is generous to all who are willing to open their hearts and minds to what she offers, and today she pours her gifts into the auto mechanic who analyzes car problems with uncommon intelligence, the grandmother who knows the truth about what makes people tick, the elementary school teacher who can both instruct and inspire her students, the counselor who shows real knowledge about the workings of human relationships, the attorney who has a passion for justice, the high-school student who resists peer pressure, and the entrepreneur who finds that she or he can do well by doing good.

Wisdom will speak only "noble things," and all the words of her mouth "are righteous; there is nothing twisted or crooked in them" (Prov 8:6, 8). Her gifts are "better than jewels," she says, "and all that you may desire cannot compare with her" (Prov 8:11). When we look at ourselves, and at people around us, we realize that wisdom is reserved not only for people with the most distinguished diplomas and powerful professions—in fact, the nightly news reveals that there is plenty of folly and foolishness at the highest levels of academics, business, and politics. True insight is available to all people everywhere who are willing to open their hearts and their minds to the wisdom of God. "I love those who love me," says Wisdom, "and those who seek me diligently find me" (Prov 8:17).

Such people are smart bricks in the "spiritual house" that God is building in the world. They are "living stones," building blocks that are "chosen and precious in God's sight" (1 Pet 2:4–5). They are like the smart bricks that actually exist in the world of modern high-tech construction: building materials that can serve as a very good metaphor for the people of God. Invented by Professor Chang Liu at the University of Illinois, the smart brick is filled with electronic sensors that can continuously monitor the structural health of a building. Such a smart brick can be a real asset in terms of routine maintenance and safety in emergencies, because it allows engineers and emergency personnel to acquire real-time information on a building's structural integrity.[1]

Smart bricks are a good image for us to keep in mind as we ponder our role as people of God in the world today. Smart bricks understand how the world is put together, because they are in touch with Wisdom, who stood beside God "like a master worker" in the original ordering of creation (Prov 8:30). She was created by the LORD at the beginning of God's work, "at the first, before the beginning of the earth" (Prov 8:22–23). Here, Wisdom is an agent of God the Creator, says Old Testament professor Walter Brueggemann, ordering creation in such a way that it is "permitted to function in abundant, life-giving ways."[2] Smart bricks are committed to building up, not breaking down. They are constructive, not destructive. They stand together and work together, instead of splitting apart and shattering the efforts of others. They join the wisdom of God in rejoicing in God's "inhabited world and delighting in the human race" (Prov 8:31).

Many people see a connection between Divine Wisdom and Jesus, the one who is the Word of God in human form. Wisdom was present at the beginning of God's work, and "in the beginning was the Word, and the Word was with God, and the Word was God." Wisdom was a master worker, and in similar manner "all things came into being through [the Word]" (John 1:1, 3). Wisdom delighted in the human race, and "God so

1. Baard, "Smart bricks, or a dumb idea?" § 1.
2. Brueggemann, *An Introduction to the Old Testament*, 315.

loved the world that he gave his only Son, so that everyone who believes in him may not perish but may have eternal life" (John 3:16). Although Divine Wisdom and Jesus the Word are not identical, they share the mission of helping the human race.

Each of us, in our own ways, can follow the example of Wisdom and Jesus in building up instead of breaking down. We can be constructive, not destructive. We can stand together and work together, instead of splitting apart and shattering each other's efforts. This passage is one of the Bible's greatest hits because it tells us that Divine Wisdom shares her life-giving gifts with us—gifts of intelligence, truth, instruction, knowledge, justice, and righteousness. With the Wisdom of God inside us, we can build a better world. One brick at a time.

Questions:

1. Where do you see examples of Divine Wisdom in the people around you?
2. What does it mean to you to be a "smart brick" in God's spiritual house?
3. How do you try to follow the example of Divine Wisdom and Jesus?

21

Ecclesiastes 1:1–14

ECCLESIASTES IS A WISDOM book which contains the words of "the Teacher" or "the Preacher," identified as "the son of David, king in Jerusalem" (Eccl 1:1). The book addresses the ultimate questions of life and death, beginning with the observation that "all is vanity" (Eccl 1:2). The Teacher—called *Qoheleth* in Hebrew—takes a cold-eyed look at the world, and he certainly isn't the philosopher to consult if you need some cheering up. "All is vanity," Ecclesiastes insists: All is worthless, meaningless, absurd; as solid as vapor, fog, and steam. The Teacher surveys society and spots extreme pride in human appearance and accomplishments. He looks around and sees narcissism—defined as excessive self-love and admiration.

According to *Psychology Today*, narcissism can range from an annoying tendency to a serious clinical disorder. We aren't talking just about people who imitate the character Narcissus, the handsome young man of Greek mythology who withdrew from the world, content to gaze forever at his own reflection in a pool of water. People with this kind of vanity are pathetic but basically harmless. No, real-life narcissists desperately need other people to validate their own worth. "It's not so much being liked," says Roy Baumeister, a social psychologist at Florida State University. "It's much more important to be admired. Studies have shown narcissists are willing to sacrifice being liked if they think it's necessary to be admired."[1] Vain people want to be admired for being unique, even though Ecclesiastes knows that "there is nothing new under the sun" (Eccl 1:9).

---

1. Vogel, "A field guide to narcissism," § 1.

This craving for admiration is a red flag, one of the clearest warning signs of narcissism. So how can we spot this tendency in ourselves and in the people around us, and what can we do about it? We can take instruction from the Teacher of Ecclesiastes, who examines all the human deeds that are done under the sun and concludes, "All is vanity and a chasing after wind" (Eccl 1:14). At first glance, this seems to be a depressing picture of human life. It's hard to accept that absolutely *everything* is meaningless. But on a deeper level, the Teacher is saying that we do not gain self-worth from our accomplishments. "What do people gain from all the toil at which they toil under the sun?" he asks. *Nothing.* "A generation goes, and a generation comes, but the earth remains forever" (Eccl 1:3-4). He also implies that our self-worth does not come from our possessions. "All things are wearisome; more than one can express; the eye is not satisfied with seeing, or the ear filled with hearing" (Eccl 1:8). We look around at things we want, and our appetite is rarely satisfied. Ecclesiastes says that we shouldn't be admired for our human deeds or our possessions. Instead, our worth comes completely from being children of God. Everything else is vanity.

In addition, we cannot remain at the center of things forever. "The people of long ago are not remembered," says the Teacher, "nor will there be any remembrance of people yet to come by those who come after them" (Eccl 1:11). Narcissists don't like this, because they like to be seen and remembered. The Teacher says, "I saw all the deeds that are done under the sun; and see, all is vanity and a chasing after wind" (Eccl 1:14). The truth of human life is that our days are numbered, and our deeds and accomplishments are going to fade away when we're gone. Ecclesiastes knows that the cycles of nature will continue whether we are living in the world or not: "The sun rises and the sun goes down . . . The wind blows . . . All streams run to the sea . . . they continue to flow" (Eccl 1:5-7).

Scripture says that we're created from the dust of the earth, and to dust we shall return. In the first of his letters, Peter says, "All flesh is like grass . . . The grass withers, and the flower falls, but the word of the Lord endures forever" (1 Pet 1:24-25). Both the Teacher and Peter have a profound insight into the transience of human life—we grow and wither like grass, while the word of the Lord endures. Moving beyond vanity begins when people discover that they cannot find self-worth in accomplishments or possessions, nor can they remain at the center of things forever. Only when narcissists ask why their lives feel so empty do they take a step toward truly life-giving relationships with God and with the people around them.

Ecclesiastes 1:1–14

Jesus teaches us that God—not ourselves—should be at the center of our lives, and that the greatest of commandments is to "love the Lord your God with all your heart, and with all your soul, and with all your mind." He goes on to say that a second commandment is like it: "You shall love your neighbor as yourself" (Matt 22:37, 39). To focus on God and neighbor is the opposite of narcissism and is also the antidote to vanity. This passage from Ecclesiastes is one of the Bible's greatest hits because it teaches us that the solution to narcissism isn't self-hatred. Instead, it's a set of healthy relationships with God, with self, and with the people of God around us. In a world of vanity, vapor, and steam, this is where we can find a solid, meaningful life.

Questions:

1. Where do you see narcissists in the world, and what harm do they do?
2. Why are accomplishments and possessions a poor measure of self-worth?
3. How are we helped by focusing on relationships with God and neighbor?

22

Song of Solomon 2:8–14

THE SONG OF SOLOMON, also known as "Song of Songs," is a book of love poetry with two main characters: The female lover and the male lover. Their expressions of human love are meant to reveal the presence of God in all of life, even the most personal and intimate of encounters. Still, the Song is controversial. "The poem describes two young lovers aching with desire," writes Lisa Miller in *Newsweek*. "The obsession is mutual, carnal, complete." The man studies his lover's eyes, hair, neck and breasts, until he arrives at "the mountain of myrrh" (Song 4:6). "You are altogether beautiful, my love," he says; "there is no flaw in you" (Song 4:7). The female lover responds in kind. "My beloved thrust his hand into the opening," she says, "and my inmost being yearned for him" (Song 5:4). "Biblical interpreters have endeavored through the millennia to temper its heat by arguing that it means more than it appears to mean," writes Miller. "It's about God's love for Israel, they have said; or, it's about Jesus' love for the church. But whatever other layers it may contain, the Song is on its face an ancient piece of erotica, a celebration of the fulfillment of sexual desire."[1]

Some Jews and Christians have objected to the book, even seeking to remove it from the Bible. But the Song of Solomon is not a dirty book. Instead, the passionate longings of its characters give us important insights into the nature of human desire and the nature of God's desire for us. This song is filled with vivid descriptions of the human body, intimate relationships, and sensual love. "The voice of my beloved!" says the female lover. "Look, he comes, leaping upon the mountains, bounding over the hills. My

1. Miller, "What the Bible Really Says About Sex," § 1.

beloved is like a gazelle or a young stag. Look, there he stands behind our wall, gazing in at the windows" (Song 2:8–9). You can hear her desire and her admiration. Then her beloved speaks and says to her, "Arise, my love, my fair one, and come away; for now the winter is past, the rain is over and gone" (Song 2:10–11). It is springtime, and this young man's thoughts are turning to love. The flowers are appearing on the earth, the time of singing has come, the fig tree is putting forth fruit, the vines are in fragrant blossom (Song 2:12–13). Such a sensual scene: bright flowers, sweet songs, succulent fruits, and fragrant vines. The richness of life and love could hardly be more obvious or desirable. "With springtime," says biblical scholar Renita Weems, "comes belief in new adventures, new possibilities, and, most of all, a new outlook on life."[2]

These are the promises of the Song of Solomon, including both the sensual and the spiritual. When we dare to open this book, we discover new adventures, possibilities, and outlooks. *First, adventure.* In the book of Genesis, Abraham sends a servant back to his homeland to find a wife for his son Isaac. The servant travels many miles, and at the well of a city he prays that a young woman will offer him water. When Rebekah appears and does this, the servant knows that his prayers have been answered. He asks for the permission of Rebekah's family, and then he takes her home, where Isaac takes "Rebekah, and she became his wife; and he loved her" (Gen 24:67). The journey of God's people, from the book of Genesis onward, has always included the adventure of entering new territory, seeking and finding partners, falling in love, and building a family.

Next, possibilities. Jesus knew that many religious people have a problem with the sensual parts of life. But he was no ascetic—he ate and drank with friends, and enjoyed the pleasures of touch, taste, smell, and sight. When his critics saw him eating and drinking, they said, "Look, a glutton and a drunkard, a friend of tax collectors and sinners!" (Matt 11:19). But Jesus understood that there were possibilities for connections across dinner tables, so he practiced radical hospitality, eating with outcasts so that they could discover God's desire for a relationship with them. God did not send Jesus into the world to condemn the world, but to save it (John 3:17). The Song of Solomon is a colorful picture of healthy human connections—physical, emotional and spiritual.

Finally, a new outlook on life. When we imagine Christ leaping upon the mountains, bounding over the hills, we see a Messiah who has a burning

---

2. Weems, "The Song of Songs," 393.

desire to be with us. When we read of a servant crossing a desert to find a wife, or a Savior reaching across a table to welcome us, we understand that our God is doing everything that can be done to make a connection with us. The result is a new outlook on life, one in which we see ourselves as people who are desired by Jesus Christ and Almighty God. Not just accepted, but *deeply desired*. We are their love, their fair one, the one they invite to "come away" and enjoy eternal life. They have a passion for each one of us, and a hunger to be intimately involved with us. This passage from the Song of Solomon is one of the Bible's greatest hits because it beckons us with the words, "Let me see your face, let me hear your voice" (Song 2:14). We are invited to show ourselves, speak, and spend our life with God. The Lord wants us to surrender to this desire and to live with God forever.

Questions:

1. How does human desire reflect God's desire for us?
2. What is the importance of adventure in the life of faith?
3. Where do you see new possibilities in your relationship with God?

23

Isaiah 56:1–8

THE BOOK OF ISAIAH is the first of the prophetic books which make up the final section of the Old Testament. In each of these books, God spoke through the prophets to reveal the divine will to the people of Israel, and to call people to return to God's way. Although the prophets sometimes spoke about the future, they are not to be seen primarily as fortune-tellers. Instead, they are best understood as truth-tellers, bringing words of challenge and comfort to the people of God.

Isaiah lived in the eighth century before the birth of Christ, during the reigns of King Ahaz and possibly King Hezekiah. The first part of the book, through chapter 39, pronounces judgment and doom, while the end of the book, chapters 40 through 66, contains prophecies of hope and restoration, including the words: "Maintain justice, and do what is right, for soon my salvation will come, and my deliverance be revealed" (Isa 56:1). Chapter 56 is in this final portion of the book, and it may have been written by a follower of Isaiah in the sixth century before Christ. The chapter addresses "a dispute about inclusion and exclusion in the community," writes Walter Brueggemann, "after the great restoration from exile had been accomplished."[1]

The chapter speaks of God's covenant being extended, for the first time, beyond the people of Israel. "Happy is the mortal who does this," said Isaiah, "the one who holds it fast, who keeps the sabbath, not profaning it, and refrains from doing any evil" (Isa 56:2). *Any* mortal who keeps the sabbath and refrains from evil can now be part of God's covenant community. This insight by Isaiah was revolutionary, because the purity code of

---

1. Brueggemann, *An Introduction to the Old Testament*, 170.

Deuteronomy excluded two particular categories of people: Eunuchs and foreigners. Deuteronomy said that no one who has been castrated "shall be admitted to the assembly of the Lord," nor shall any "Ammonite or Moabite" (Deut 23:1, 3).

But Isaiah offered a new vision of community, one in which all people who honor the Lord in their actions are to be included. Speaking through Isaiah, God said, "To the eunuchs who keep my sabbaths, who choose the things that please me and hold fast my covenant . . . I will give them an everlasting name that shall not be cut off" (Isa 56:4–5). The tragedy of the eunuch was that he was cut off, literally—no chance of having children to carry on his name. But now, if the eunuch was faithful, God would give him an everlasting name. "And the foreigners who join themselves to the Lord, to minister to him," says Isaiah, "these I will bring to my holy mountain, and make them joyful in my house of prayer" (Isa 56:6–7). That's remarkable, isn't it? Previously excluded people are now included, because they honor God in their actions and relationships. They are accepted because God wants to be worshiped in "a house of prayer for all peoples" (Isa 56:7). Old Testament scholar Brevard Childs says that this verse "removes any doubt that God's purpose for his house is directed to all peoples without restriction."[2] God's house is now open to *everyone* who keeps the sabbath and holds fast to the covenant.

What a radical shift this was. Suddenly, the community of faith was not limited to people of the same nationality, and being admitted to the assembly of the Lord did not require being a man or a woman in a traditional family. Through Isaiah, God called for barriers to fall in the religious community, which began a movement of inclusiveness that only accelerated when Jesus began his gracious and loving ministry. A strong connection exists between Isaiah and Jesus, since people often see Jesus as the fulfillment of Isaiah's prophecies (e.g. Isa 7:14), and Isaiah is the prophet that Jesus quotes the most (eight times). "Many of Jesus' miracles are worked for outsiders," writes historian Garry Wills. The miracles of Jesus teach lessons about the reign of God, and "one of the main lessons is that people should not be separated into classes of the clean and unclean, the worthy and the unworthy, the respectable and the unrespectable."[3] Jesus himself fulfilled the prophecy of Isaiah, "Thus says the Lord God, who gathers the outcasts of Israel, I will gather others to them besides those already gathered" (Isa 56:8).

---

2. Childs, *Isaiah*, 459.
3. Wills, *What Jesus Meant*, 29–30.

Isaiah 56:1–8

This movement of inclusiveness matters deeply to God, and it is found throughout the whole of Scripture. "The Sages noted the repeated emphasis on the stranger in biblical law," said Rabbi Jonathan Sacks. "Not only must the stranger not be wronged; he or she must be included in the positive welfare provisions of Israelite/Jewish society. But the law goes beyond this; the stranger must be loved."[4] That's tough. Love the person who is not like us, who has a different skin color, sexual orientation, or cultural background. The challenge of inclusiveness was lifted up first by the prophet Isaiah, and it continues to be a goal for people of faith today. The words "my house shall be called a house of prayer for all peoples" (Isa 56:7) is one of the Bible's greatest hits, because it calls us to focus our efforts on welcoming and including all of God's children in the community of faith.

Questions:

1. Which groups are still excluded from many faith communities, and why?
2. What does it mean to you to be in a "house of prayer for all peoples"?
3. What are the challenges we face when we try to love the stranger?

---

4. Sacks, "Loving the Stranger," § 1.

24

Jeremiah 31:31–34

THE PROPHET JEREMIAH CALLED the people of Israel to repent from their unfaithfulness, and announced judgment because they had broken their covenant with God. He prepared the people for exile in Babylon, but also anticipated that they would return and that God would make a new covenant with them. But what is a covenant? The word is ancient and biblical, and it describes a promise-based relationship. Today, the phrase "covenant of marriage" is used to describe a relationship based on vows, one in which two people promise to be faithful to each other "for better for worse, for richer for poorer, in sickness and in health." God uses some of the language of marriage when God says that the new covenant "will not be like the covenant that I made with their ancestors when I took them by the hand to bring them out of the land of Egypt—a covenant that they broke, though I was their husband, says the LORD" (Jer 31:32).

Such promise-based relationships have their origin in the covenant God made with Abraham, "I will make my covenant between me and you, and will make you exceedingly numerous" (Gen 17:2). God was faithful to this covenant with the people of Israel, saying, "I will take you as my people, and I will be your God. You shall know that I am the LORD your God, who has freed you from the burdens of the Egyptians" (Exo 6:7). Later, God extended the covenant to "the foreigners who join themselves to the LORD" (Isa 56:6). In effect, this covenant was a deal in which God said, "I will be your God, and you will be my people. I'll love, comfort, honor, and keep you. Forsaking all others, I'll be faithful to you forever. All I ask is that you do the same for me."

Jeremiah 31:31-34

Well, you can guess what happened: God remained faithful, but the people did not. They broke the deal and worshiped other gods, despite the fact that God loved them like a husband loves a wife. Fortunately, God did not abandon the people of Israel, but instead chose to "make a new covenant with the house of Israel and the house of Judah . . . I will put my law within them [says the Lord], and I will write it on their hearts; and I will be their God, and they shall be my people" (Jer 31:31, 33). When the people broke the covenant, God offered a new deal. It came as a surprise, bringing the powerful love of God into the very center of human life. The people had done nothing to deserve it—it was a completely free gift, a gift of grace.

There are times when we all need a new deal. Maybe we have broken a promise to ourselves and engaged in self-destructive behavior. Maybe we have betrayed a spouse or a friend, and fractured a relationship. The old deal is shattered and we need something to help us to start over. The American people discovered this in the 1930s and 40s, when President Franklin Delano Roosevelt offered his "Fireside Chats," radio broadcasts that were offered in an informal, conversational tone. Until that time, presidents were largely cut off from the American people, and they seemed to be very distant from the average person. But then FDR, who had campaigned on a "New Deal for the American people," spoke with sincerity and compassion about a New Deal that would replace the old deal which produced the Great Depression. After his first chat, "he was inundated with fan mail from listeners who felt they now knew him intimately."[1]

Into our spiritual depression, God promises a New Deal. Speaking to the people of Israel and to us, God says, "I will put my law within them, and I will write it on their hearts." God promises to move the law from a piece of paper to the center of the human heart. "I will be their God, and they shall be my people," says the Lord (Jer 31:33). The loving bond between God and people will be renewed, like a renewal of vows between spouses. "No longer shall they teach one another, or say to each other, 'Know the Lord,' for they shall all know me," says God. Knowledge of God will suddenly shift inward, and all of us will have a deep and personal relationship with God. "I will forgive their iniquity," promises God (Jer 31:34). With this new relationship will come forgiveness of sin and a chance to move forward, fully accepted by God.

For Christians, the terms of this New Deal are made clear in the one who put God's new covenant in human form: Jesus Christ. The law was

1. Latson, "How FDR's Radio Voice Solved a Banking Crisis," § 1.

given through Moses, says the Gospel according to John, "grace and truth came through Jesus Christ. No one has ever seen God. It is God the only Son, who is close to the Father's heart, who has made him known" (John 1:17–18). When we believe in Jesus, we enter into a new covenant with God. We accept his promise of forgiveness and eternal life, and offer our own promise to follow Jesus in faith, "for better for worse, for richer for poorer, in sickness and in health." This passage from Jeremiah is one of the Bible's greatest hits because it promises us that God is always reaching out to us in love, inviting us to enter into a deep and personal relationship with God, one that is truly heart-to-heart.

Questions:

1. What does the "covenant of marriage" mean to you?
2. When one party breaks a deal, how can the relationship be restored?
3. How does Jeremiah's new covenant connect with Jesus, if at all?

25

Lamentations 3:22–33

LAMENTATIONS IS LOCATED IMMEDIATELY after the book of Jeremiah in the Christian Old Testament because of the traditional understanding that the prophet Jeremiah was the author of the book. But in the Jewish Bible, Lamentations is in the third and final section, grouped with other writings. The book is a series of five expressions of grief called laments, and in 1923 Thomas Chisholm wrote the hymn "Great Is Thy Faithfulness" as a meditation on Lamentations. Chisholm was born in 1866 in Kentucky, and was ordained into the Methodist ministry at age thirty-six. Shortly after his ordination, his health failed and he had to leave the ministry. He moved to Indiana and then New Jersey, where he opened an insurance office. He began writing poetry and sent a number of poems to William Runyan, a friend and colleague in ministry. Runyan wrote the tune called "Faithfulness," hoping that it would carry the message of the poem "in a worthy way."[1]

The well-known refrain of the hymn says: "Great is thy faithfulness! Great is thy faithfulness! / Morning by morning, new mercies I see. / All I have needed thy hand hath provided. / Great is thy faithfulness, Lord unto me!" Chisholm's words are a poetic adaptation of Lamentations 3:22–23: "The steadfast love of the LORD never ceases, his mercies never come to an end; they are new every morning; great is your faithfulness."

The hymn is one of the few hymns among the 1200 poems written by Chisholm that is still in use today. He wrote it as a testimony to God's faithfulness through his very ordinary life. "My income has not been large

---

1. McKim, *The Presbyterian Hymnal Companion*, 197–98.

at any time due to impaired health in the earlier years which has followed me on until now," he wrote toward the end of his life. "Although I must not fail to record here the unfailing faithfulness of a covenant-keeping God and that he has given me many wonderful displays of his providing care, for which I am filled with astonishing gratefulness."[2] Believing that "the steadfast love of the LORD never ceases," Chisholm addressed God directly with the words, "Great is thy faithfulness."

Since God's mercies never come to an end, the writer of Lamentations goes on to say, "The LORD is my portion . . . therefore I will hope in him" (Lam 3:24). In this case, writes professor of Old Testament Kathleen O'Connor, "hope is a decision of the speaker based on remembrance of divine mercy."[3] Lamentations goes on to affirm that "the LORD is good to those who wait for him, to the soul that seeks him" (Lam 3:25). But a life of seeking God is no guarantee of freedom from suffering. "It is good for one to bear the yoke in youth," he writes, "to sit alone in silence when the Lord has imposed it, to put one's mouth to the dust (there may yet be hope), to give one's cheek to the smiter, and be filled with insults" (Lam 3:27–30). The writer's "waiting here is expectant, and it is filled with suffering," says O'Connor.[4]

Not surprisingly, many Christians associate these verses with Jesus and his suffering. After all, he was the one who bore a cross and was "filled with insults." But the passage ends on a more hopeful note, with the assurance that "the Lord will not reject forever. Although he causes grief, he will have compassion according to the abundance of his steadfast love; for he does not willingly afflict or grieve anyone" (Lam 3:31–33). A balance is struck in these verses between the God who "causes grief" and the God "who will have compassion." In the end, God may be the cause of grief, but God does not "willingly afflict or grieve anyone." Perhaps God allows suffering to occur, but God does not will people to suffer.

This chapter of Lamentations raises important questions about divine power. O'Connor asks, "Is God the source of or able to prevent historical tragedy? Or is God in some sense limited by the world and its ways?" The writer of Lamentations may be pointing to "a God who suffers with, who empathizes with, who is pained by the destruction of the people."[5] This

---

2. White, "Ordinary man with simple faith wrote extraordinary hymn," § 1.
3. O'Connor, "The Book of Lamentations," 1051.
4. O'Connor, 1051.
5. O'Connor, 1058.

understanding of God is certainly revealed in the life of Jesus, one who suffered terribly in his own life, and who felt compassion for those in pain around him. In the Gospel of Mark, Jesus crossed the Sea of Galilee by boat, and when "he went ashore, he saw a great crowd; and he had compassion for them" (Mark 6:34). The word compassion comes from the Latin *com-*, "with," and *pati*, "to suffer." When Jesus shows compassion, he literally "suffers with" the people around him.

The Book of Lamentations does not answer the question of how a good God allows pain and suffering to exist in the world, but it does affirm that "the steadfast love of the Lord never ceases, his mercies never come to an end; they are new every morning; great is your faithfulness" (Lam 3:22–23). This passage is one of the Bible's greatest hits because it tells us that God's steadfast love and mercy are eternal. In a world of suffering and lamentation, we can gain comfort from the knowledge that God suffers alongside us, and that God's faithfulness to us is always great.

Questions:

1. Where do you see signs of the faithfulness of God?
2. What is the significance of suffering in the life of faith?
3. How does the love of God help you to cope with pain?

26

Ezekiel 37:1–14

IN 1954, A SINGER named Big Joe Turner gathered with a group of rhythm-and-blues musicians in New York City. In the offices of Atlantic Records, they pushed the furniture to the walls and recorded a song called "Shake, Rattle and Roll." It was quickly picked up and recorded by Bill Haley and His Comets, and then by Elvis Presley. The song became Haley's first gold record, a best-seller for Decca in 1954, and an important piece of rock history.[1] Six decades later, people still Shake, Rattle and Roll.

But Big Joe Turner was not the creator of this distinctive sound. Going back many centuries, we find the prophet Ezekiel, taken into exile in the city of Babylon more than five hundred years before the birth of Christ. While in captivity, the prophet sees seven visions which include messages of judgment on Israel because of their idolatry, messages of judgment on the other nations of the world, and promises of future blessings for the people of Israel. Sadly, the thirty-seventh chapter of Ezekiel begins in a lifeless place. The passage seems more like a judgment than a blessing when the prophet reports that the hand and the spirit of God "set me down in the middle of a valley; it was full of bones. He led me all around them; there were very many lying in the valley, and they were very dry" (Ezek 37:1–2). The "Valley of Dry Bones," writes Walter Brueggemann, is "a metaphor for Israel in exile with no prospect for the future."[2]

Bones. Dry bones. No signs of life. No rock-and-roll drum beats. God says to Ezekiel, "Mortal, can these bones live?" And the prophet, seeing no

1. Ward, "The Big Man Behind 'Shake, Rattle and Roll,'" § 1.
2. Brueggemann, *An Introduction to the Old Testament*, 200.

evidence of vitality, simply says, "O Lord God, you know" (Ezek 37:3). For Ezekiel, life for these bones does not seem possible. They are dry, and we all know what dry feels like. Dry is when you are finding no career path in your 20s, struggling to get pregnant in your 30s, feeling distant from your spouse in your 40s, losing your job in your 50s, worrying about retirement in your 60s, and suffering the death of your partner in your 70s. Mortal, can these bones live? It doesn't seem possible. The bones are so dry.

But the prophet knows that nothing is impossible with God. "O Lord God," he says, "you know." God gives a command to Ezekiel, "Prophesy to these bones, and say to them: O dry bones, hear the word of the Lord" (Ezek 37:3-4). The prophet is told to deliver the word of God to the dry bones because this word has the power to create something new, to bring life to the dead. Since the beginning of time, God's word has shown creative, life-giving power. In the first chapter of Genesis, God says, "Let there be light," and there *is* light—the word of God creates a new reality, bringing light into darkness (Gen 1:3). Through the prophet Isaiah, God promises that "my word . . . shall not return to me empty, but it shall accomplish that for which I purpose" (Isa 55:11). "In the beginning was the Word," says the Gospel of John, "and the Word was with God, and the Word was God . . . All things came into being through him" (John 1:1, 3).

Throughout the Bible, the Word of God has life-giving power, and Ezekiel is willing to trust this Word. In the middle of his own dry, dusty, lifeless experience in exile, he is willing to put his faith in the God who says to the bones, "I will cause breath to enter you, and you shall live . . . and you shall know that I am the Lord" (Ezek 37:5-6). God promises to cause breath to enter the bones—literally, God causes *ruah* to enter. *Ruah* is the Hebrew word for "breath," and it also means wind and spirit. *Ruah* is the breath that inspires God's creative words (Psalm 33:6). *Ruah* is the "breath of life" that is snuffed out by the great flood (Gen 6:17). *Ruah* is the "wind from God" that sweeps over the face of the waters at the beginning of creation (Gen 1:2). *Ruah* is the "holy spirit" that we need in order to feel the presence of God (Psalm 51:11). God puts it into us so that we can live. Ezekiel reports, "suddenly there was a noise, a rattling, and the bones came together, bone to its bone" (Ezek 37:7). Through the power of God, the bones begin to Shake, Rattle and Roll.

God says to Ezekiel, "Mortal, these bones are the whole house of Israel. They say, 'Our bones are dried up, and our hope is lost; we are cut off completely'" (Ezek 37:11). God commands Ezekiel to assure them that he will open their graves, bring them back to life, and return them to their homeland in Israel. "I will put my spirit within you," promises God, "and you shall live, and I will place you on your own soil; then you shall know that I, the Lord, have spoken and will act" (Ezek 37:14).

This promise is true for us as well, when our bones are dried up and our hope is lost. This passage is one of the Bible's greatest hits because it shows us that God's Word and God's breath-wind-spirit can give us new life, as individuals and as communities. When dry bones begin to rattle and join together, we discover together that hope is stronger than despair, death is never final, and sadness can give way to joy. Shake, Rattle and Roll. Much more than a song, it's a sign that God is always raising us to new life.

Questions:

1. When has your life felt like dry bones?
2. How have you experienced the life-giving power of God's Word, if at all?
3. Where do you see a connection between breath, wind and spirit?

27

Daniel 7:9–14

THIS BOOK IS NAMED for the prophet Daniel, who was taken into exile in Babylon when King Nebuchadnezzar besieged Jerusalem. Stress was high for Daniel and his fellow Israelites, and many wondered what it meant to stay true to the God of Israel in a place so far from home. "By the rivers of Babylon," they lamented in Psalm 137, "there we sat down and there we wept . . . How could we sing the Lord's song in a foreign land?" (Psalm 137:1, 4). Daniel was promoted in the king's court for interpreting dreams, but was later thrown into a lion's den for persisting in prayer. Then he had "a dream and visions of his head as he lay in bed" (Dan 7:1). His vision was of four great beasts representing kingdoms of the world, along with an "Ancient One" (Dan 7:9, 13).

Daniel found hope for a difficult time by focusing on the end of God's story. In his vision, God is the "Ancient One" who sits on a throne blazing with fiery flames. God's clothing is white as snow, his hair is like pure wool, and a stream of fire flows out from his presence. The court around him sits in judgment, and the divine record books are opened. This is an "apocalyptic vision"—an unveiling or revelation of God at the very end of time. God quickly renders judgment on the empires of the world, destroying one and leaving the other three powerless. Then appears "one like a human being coming with the clouds of heaven" (Dan 7:13). God gives to this son of man "dominion and glory and kingship, that all peoples, nations, and languages should serve him . . . and his kingship is one that shall never be destroyed" (Dan 7:14). For Daniel, this vision was a perfect moment—one that gave him hope for the future. It revealed that *God is always working to bring order out of chaos and victory out of defeat.*

The same is true for us. No matter how many horrors confront us in the news, God is always working with God's people, in every time and place and situation. The exiles in Babylon might have understood Daniel's "one like a human" to be the angel Michael, since he does battle for Israel a little later in the book, in chapter 10. But Christians see Jesus Christ as the Son of Man, the one who comes at the end of time as "King of kings and Lord of lords," a rider on a white horse who judges in righteousness and makes war with evil (Rev 19:11–16). He is "the ruler of the kings of the earth," according to the book of Revelation. "He is coming with the clouds; every eye will see him, even those who pierced him; and on his account all the tribes of the earth will wail" (Rev 1:5, 7).

For Israelite exiles in Babylon, first-century Christians in Rome, and twenty-first century men and women around the world, the message is the same: God is in control. The forces of chaos and cruelty may take an occasional battle, but they cannot win the war, because the Lord of heaven and earth is alive and well and having an ongoing impact on human life. God's son Jesus has come to us once, and he will come to us again, to wipe the tears from our eyes and establish "a new heaven and a new earth" (Rev 21:1). He comes to show us that God desires an everlasting relationship with us, one that cannot be disrupted by mourning or crying or pain . . . or even death itself.

In the end, it's all about relationships: relationships with God and with one another. A man named Eugene O'Kelly sensed this, which is why he spent so much time with friends and family during the last hundred days of his life. At age fifty-three, O'Kelly seemed to be in excellent health, traveling and working long hours. But then a visit to his doctor revealed that he had an aggressive brain cancer that would kill him in one hundred days. He had focused on building and planning for the future. "Now," he said, "I would have to learn the true value of the present." Like the prophet Daniel, O'Kelly discovered that challenging times can be the best of times. A man of faith, he decided to "unwind" relationships with people in his life, taking the time to have final conversations with those who had meant a great deal to him. He also went searching for what he called "Perfect Moments"—times of lingering over a fine meal, enjoying a deep conversation, taking the time to soak up the beauty of nature over the course of an afternoon. Then he died, reports

The New York Times, just as his doctors predicted.[1] He leaves us with the challenge of living with the end in mind, and learning the true value of the present.

Whether we have brain cancer or not, whether we are having good days or not, we can do our best to have quality conversations with family members, friends, colleagues, and neighbors. We can work on our relationship with God through regular worship and by serving others in the name of Christ. We can look to the future with confidence, trusting that our Lord is actively involved in our lives, always working for restoration and peace. Like the prophet Daniel and Eugene O'Kelly, we'll marvel at how many perfect moments we can have right now. Daniel's vision of the Ancient One is one of the Bible's greatest hits because it tells us that God is always working to bring order out of chaos and victory out of defeat, in every time and place and situation.

Questions:

1. How does a focus on the end of time give us hope for today?
2. Where do you see God working to bring order out of chaos?
3. When have you experienced "Perfect Moments" in your life?

---

1. Dean, "When cancer strikes, a high achiever plans," D7.

28

Hosea 1:2–10

Hosea was a prophet during the reigns of five kings, Uzziah through Jeroboam, and his book appears in the Bible as the first of the twelve Minor Prophets. Themes of infidelity and punishment appear throughout the book, including the opening chapter in which Hosea's marriage and children represent the unfaithfulness of Israel and God's response. At the beginning of this section, the Lord said to Hosea, "Go, take for yourself a wife of whoredom and have children of whoredom, for the land commits great whoredom by forsaking the Lord" (Hos 1:2). God wanted Hosea to create a living, breathing example of the unfaithfulness of the people of Israel. In a sense, the Lord was nominating Hosea and his family for a Darwin Award—a dubious distinction given to people who self-destruct in the most remarkable manner.

Not as glamorous as an Oscar or an Emmy, the award is named in honor of Charles Darwin, who developed the theory of natural selection. The awards commemorate those people who improve our gene pool by removing themselves from it, usually doing so in an extraordinarily stupid manner. For example, a man was crushed to death on a stairway at the Sammis Real Estate and Insurance Office in Huntington, New York, while he was stealing the office's six-hundred-pound safe. He apparently violated the cardinal rule of hauling massive objects: Never stand on a step lower than the one the safe is on. Adding insult to injury: The safe was empty at the time of the incident.[1] Any death of a human being is tragic, of course, but this one falls under the category of gallows humor. Winners of Darwin Awards

---

1. Northcutt, *The Darwin Awards II: Unnatural Selection*, 9.

are cautionary tales that remind us that life is fragile and our actions have consequences.

So why would Hosea and his family qualify for such an award? Hosea's wife Gomer conceived and bore him a son. And the LORD said to him, "Name him Jezreel; for in a little while I will punish the house of Jehu for the blood of Jezreel." When she bore a daughter, the LORD said to Hosea, "Name her Lo-ruhamah." When she had weaned Lo-ruhamah, she bore a son, and the LORD said, "Name him Lo-ammi" (Hos 1:4, 6, 9). Like other Darwin Award recipients, Hosea's tale is a story of self-destruction. Obedient to God's call to take "a wife of whoredom" (Hos 1:2), Hosea marries the prostitute Gomer and she bears three children. Since she is "an adulterous wife" (Hos 1:2, NIV), there is no guarantee that the children are part of Hosea's gene pool, which sets up the prophet and his family for mocking and abuse.

On top of this, the names of his kids are descriptive and depressing: Jezreel, Lo-ruhamah, and Lo-ammi. The daughter's name, Lo-ruhamah, means "Not pitied," since the child was to be a living reminder that the Lord no longer had pity on the house of Israel because of its sin. The second son's name, Lo-ammi, means "Not my people," and the boy was to be a stark sign of the breaking of the covenant relationship between the Lord and Israel. This remarkable behavior is initiated by God, who may be venting some anger and frustration over the fact that the people of Israel had been loving other gods. "Hosea's profound insight into God's covenant with Israel arises from his own bitter experience of his wife's infidelity," writes Old Testament Professor Gale Yee.[2]

Is Hosea being too hard on Gomer? Perhaps. But putting the prophet's personal issues aside, we have to admit that we ourselves do any number of stupid and self-destructive things in our relationship with God. We find ourselves unable to resist the lure of objects, habits, and behaviors that are harmful to ourselves and others. We make selfish choices that rupture the relationships we have with God and the people closest to us. We discover that we all need grace. And fortunately, God provides it. This passage ends with Hosea saying, "Yet the number of the people of Israel shall be like the sand of the sea . . . and in the place where it was said to them, 'You are not my people,' it shall be said to them, 'Children of the living God'" (Hos 1:10). Restoration comes not through our words and actions, but through the grace of God. Even in our times of unfaithfulness, God remains faithful to us.

---

2. Yee, "The Book of Hosea," 220.

The prophet's personal life begins with outwardly self-destructive behavior, but it ends with a vivid illustration of God's redeeming love. Hosea predicts that Israel will suffer public shame like a harlot, because it has committed adultery with the gods of Canaan. But God will lure Israel back and renew God's relationship with her, taking Israel as his wife "in righteousness and in justice, in steadfast love, and in mercy" (Hos 2:19). This isn't Darwinian—it's divine. This passage from Hosea is one of the Bible's greatest hits because it reminds us that remaining faithful to God is the best path to avoiding destruction, as well as finding safety, growth, peace, and ultimate happiness.

Questions:

1. Where are the consequences of unfaithfulness seen most clearly around you?
2. What kind of behavior is most destructive to relationships?
3. How does grace and love heal ruptures in relationships, both human and divine?

29

Joel 2:1–17

THE BOOK OF THE prophet Joel begins by describing a destructive locust attack on the country, one that was connected to the coming of the Day of the Lord. The prophet looked around and saw "a day of darkness and gloom, a day of clouds and thick darkness." Locusts were covering the land "like blackness spread upon the mountains." These devouring insects were like "a great and powerful army," and Joel predicted that "their like has never been from of old, nor will be again after them in ages to come" (Joel 2:2). The people of Israel were challenged to repent—to change their ways and return to God with fasting and mourning.

In ancient Israel, the Day of the Lord was preceded by locusts, but the national disaster could have been caused by frogs, gnats, flies, boils, or hail—whatever would get the attention of the people. Today, we might be hit hard by a flood, a drought, a power outage, a virus, or a Wall Street crash. Many times through history, reports *The Atlantic* magazine, people have looked around and felt that the end was near. In the twentieth century, science fiction writer Ray Bradbury predicted that we would have to colonize Mars because of a global nuclear war. Then, on December 21, 2012, the Mayan Apocalypse was supposed to occur. Those were bold predictions, but none of them happened. Astrophysicist Adam Riess says that "the universe has at least thirty billion good years left," and our sun should last for another four to five billion years. "As for the Earth, its life span depends on how well we take care of it."[1]

---

1. "What was the worst prediction of all time?" § 1.

With such widespread failures to predict the future accurately, what are we to make of Joel's expectation that "the day of the Lord is coming, it is near" (Joel 2:1)? This prophet called for national repentance, warning that a locust plague was a sign of the beginning of the judgment of God. But Joel's prediction was not in error, like the Mayan Apocalypse of 2012. He saw locusts and was right to call for people to respond with repentance and prayer.

The very same is true today. Regardless of the particular events going on around us, the power of the Day of the Lord is that it grabs our attention and offers us the possibility of transformation. Our challenge is to shift our focus from the outside to the inside, and to follow the guidance of Joel in making the choice to *return, learn, gather, and pray*.

First, we *return* to the God who says, "return to me with all your heart, with fasting, with weeping, and with mourning" (Joel 2:12). To return to God is to repent—to turn around and go in a new and opposite direction. Novelist Ron Rash tells haunting tales of the American South, especially the North Carolina and Tennessee mountains. "Evil always rises up," he says. "And yet there are always people who fight against it. I am fascinated by the war between what is best in our natures and what is worst."[2] When we repent, we fight against evil, return to God, and turn toward what is best inside us.

After returning, we *learn* about the nature of our God, one who is "gracious and merciful, slow to anger, and abounding in steadfast love" (Joel 2:13). These are the exact words used to describe God after the people of Israel sin by making a golden calf: God is "merciful and gracious, slow to anger, and abounding in steadfast love and faithfulness" (Exod 34:6). Merciful, not wrathful. Slow to anger, not quick to condemn. Abounding in steadfast love and faithfulness, always working for good in our lives.

Then we *gather* as God's people, knowing that a transformed life must be lived in community. "Gather the people," says Joel; "Sanctify the congregation; assemble the aged; gather the children, even infants at the breast" (Joel 2:16). Gregory Boyd is an introverted pastor who has discovered that he really needs to be with others. He is now part of an extended group of about thirty people that meets once a week. "We are made in the image of the triune God, whose essence is loving community," he concludes. "We are created for community."[3] Each of us is made in the image of the God who

---

2. Frykholm, "Countering the darkness," 10.
3. Boyd, "Created for community," 20–21.

is—in God's own self—a sacred community made up of Father, Son, and Holy Spirit.

Finally, after returning, learning, and gathering in community . . . we *pray*. Between the vestibule and the altar, Joel calls for the ministers to pray, "Spare your people, O Lord, and do not make your heritage a mockery" (Joel 2:17). Such a prayer is called an intercession—asking God to act in the lives of others. In Joel, the ministers are asking God to spare the people, but other intercessions can request healing, strength, peace, or help. In his first letter to Timothy, Paul says that intercessions should be made for everyone "so that we may lead a quiet and peaceable life in all godliness and dignity" (1 Tim 2:2). At the end of the day, we are supposed to pray for ourselves and others, asking for God to heal us and help us. Instead of feeling dismay, we pray—pray for God to transform us into the people that God wants us to be. This passage from Joel is one of the Bible's greatest hits because it speaks of a "day of the Lord" that motivates us to return, learn, gather, and pray. This is a day that leads to real change, for the better.

Questions:

1. What meaning do you attach to the Day of the Lord, in the past and today?
2. How is repentance, for you, a return to God and to what is best inside you?
3. Where do you find significance in gathering in community for prayer?

30

Amos 5:18–24

Amos was a prophet who rose out of "the shepherds of Tekoa," and he spoke "in the days of King Uzziah of Judah and in the days of King Jeroboam son of Joash of Israel" (Amos 1:1). His book begins with a series of prophetic judgments against foreign nations, and then offers words against Judah and Israel. The fifth chapter is a lament for Israel's sin, followed by the prediction that the "day of the Lord" will be a dark day (Amos 5:18). Amos announces that God despises Israel's festivals and finds no delight in its "solemn assemblies" (Amos 5:21). Offerings of grain and fatted animals are no longer acceptable to God, nor are the "noise of your songs" and "the melody of your harps" (Amos 5:22–23). Instead, says God through the prophet Amos, "let justice roll down like waters, and righteousness like an ever-flowing stream" (Amos 5:24).

Three times in the book, "Amos utilizes the defining phrase 'justice and righteousness' as the core prophetic concern," says Walter Brueggemann. "A characteristic use of this phrasing is by Martin Luther King Jr., a familiar cadence of his rhetoric later utilized in his memorial in Montgomery. This phrasing of Amos has become the impetus for prophetic faith and ground for prophetic critique of social systems that disregard and violate this most elemental command of [God]."[1] According to biographer Taylor Branch, the prophet Amos was King's favorite biblical authority on justice. In his "I Have a Dream" speech during the 1963 March on Washington, which drew 250,000 people, King said, "We will not be satisfied until justice runs down like waters and righteousness like a mighty stream." The crowd

---

1. Brueggemann, *An Introduction to the Old Testament*, 227.

responded to the emotion of the prophet Amos, and Branch reports that King could not bring himself to deliver the next line of his prepared speech. Some of the people on the platform urged him on, and the gospel singer Mahalia Jackson called out as though she were in church, "Tell 'em about the dream, Martin." Branch says that King began to preach, and his words "went beyond the limitations of language and culture to express something that was neither pure rage nor pure joy, but a universal transport of the kind that makes the blues sweet." His "Dream" message took him from Amos to Isaiah, and he ended with the words, "I have a dream that one day, every valley shall be exalted."[2]

Janis Rosheuvel, the executive for racial justice for United Methodist Women, loves the image of justice rolling down like waters and righteousness like an ever-flowing stream. "I remember a trip to Niagara Falls with friends, standing in the mist of that thunderous wonder where over six million cubic feet of water falls over the crest line every minute on average. I recall also a trip with my father to our homeland, Guyana, where we stood atop Kaieteur Falls, one of the world's highest single drop waterfall, and marveled at its majesty. Whenever I am in front of a vast body of water I am shaken by its fierceness. I am made instantly humble and afraid of water's awesome potential." Rosheuvel says that she connects the powerful flow of water to the energy needed by people of faith to bring an end to racism and white supremacy.[3] In the face of every injustice, Christians are challenged to let "justice roll down like waters" (Amos 5:24).

But what exactly does Amos mean by justice? "When we hear the word 'justice' we may think of a criminal getting the punishment he deserves," writes pastor Steve Hollaway. "But the Hebrew word for justice, *mishpat*, has as its root meaning fairness and equity. When it is applied to criminal cases, justice in the Old Testament means that the judge does not take bribes and does not treat the poor worse than the rich. Most of the time, the word *mishpat* has to do with justice for those we might call underprivileged: widows, orphans, immigrants, and the poor." If we fail to show fairness to any underprivileged or marginalized people, we are failing to do justice, and the same is true if we defer to privileged or well-connected people. Likewise, the word righteousness is often misunderstood. "We probably think of righteousness in terms of personal morality," says Hollaway. "But the Hebrew word *tzadeqah* is something very different... In the

---

2. Branch, *Parting the Waters: America in the King Years 1954–63*, 881–82.
3. Rosheuvel, "Let Justice Roll Down Like Waters," § 1.

Old Testament it means something more like living in a right relationship, treating everyone with fairness, generosity, and equity."[4] Justice is taking action to make things fair, while righteousness is making an effort to live in right relationship.

Both *mishpat* and *tzadeqah* are at the heart of social justice, which is why Amos challenged the people of his day to "let justice roll down like waters, and righteousness like an ever-flowing stream" (Amos 5:24). His words continue to push us to make things fair in our society and to live in right relationship with one another—a challenge that stands before us in every time and place and situation. This passage is one of the Bible's greatest hits because its call to justice and righteousness will continue to thunder in our ears, like the mighty waters of Niagara and Kaieteur Falls.

Questions:

1. What feelings arise in you when you see rolling, flowing waters?
2. How are you challenged to practice justice in daily life?
3. Where can you improve, in your life, "right relationship" with God and others?

---

4. Hollaway, "Let Justice and Righteousness Flow," § 1.

31

Obadiah 10–16

THE BOOK OF OBADIAH is the shortest book in the Old Testament, just a single chapter in length. Because the prophet Obadiah frequently mentions Jerusalem, Judah, and Zion, he was probably working in the southern kingdom of Judah. His name means "servant of the Lord," but nothing is known of his personal life and he is never quoted in the New Testament. In the book, the kingdom of Edom and its northern neighbor Judah are portrayed as brothers, with a sibling rivalry like that of Esau and Jacob, grounded in the Book of Genesis.

The dating of the prophecy is difficult to determine, although it seems to follow an Edomite assault on Jerusalem, described in Obadiah 10–14. As a result of this assault, God offers this pronouncement concerning Edom: "I will surely make you least among the nations, you shall be utterly despised" (Obad 2). This punishment is based on the violence and inhumanity that Edom showed in its attack on Jerusalem. "For the slaughter and violence done to your brother Jacob, shame shall cover you, and you shall be cut off forever. On the day that you stood aside, on the day that strangers carried off his wealth, and foreigners entered his gates and cast lots for Jerusalem, you too were like one of them" (Obad 10–11). In particular, Edom is criticized for acting as "one of them"—as one of Judah's enemies—when Edom should have treated Judah as kin (Deut 23:7).

God's judgment, according to Obadiah, is tied to three particular failures by Edom. *First: Gloating.* "But you should not have gloated over your brother on the day of his misfortune" (Obad 12). *Second: Looting.* "You should not have looted his goods on the day of his calamity" (Obad 13).

Third: Mistreating fugitives and survivors. "You should not have stood at the crossings to cut off his fugitives; you should not have handed over his survivors on the day of distress" (Obad 14). Because of these crimes, "the day of the Lord is near against all the nations," says Obadiah. "As you have done, it shall be done to you; your deeds shall return on your own head" (Obad 15). Edom is forced to face the logical consequences of its actions and be annihilated, in line with the words of Jesus, "the measure you give will be the measure you get" (Matt 7:2).

So, given the existence of hostility between close neighbors—in the ancient world and today—what can we learn from Obadiah about standards for behavior? Some of the lessons of this book fall into the Christian tradition of "just war theory." According to the thirteenth century thinker St. Thomas Aquinas, at least three conditions must be satisfied in order for a war to be considered "just": It must be waged by lawful public authority in defense of the common good; it must be waged for a just cause; and it must be waged with the right intention—not vengefully nor to inflict harm.[1]

Was the assault of Edom on Jerusalem a "just war"? Clearly, it was not. The attack violated a number of standards for acceptable warfare. *In a just war, looting is not allowed.* "Private property must be respected and may only be taken when necessary to conduct the war," writes Catholic Brother Lawrence Mary. "Looting is not justified."[2] Edom violated this standard when it "looted [Judah's] goods on the day of his calamity" (Obad 13).

In a just war, there is no mistreating of fugitives and survivors. "Prisoners of war should not be tortured or placed as human shields to protect one's own troops," says Brother Mary. "Citizens must never be deliberately targeted. When prisoners are taken, they must not be harmed even if the enemy fails to make promised concessions or violates previous agreements."[3] Edom violated this standard when it "stood at the crossings to cut off [Judah's] fugitives; you should not have handed over his survivors on the day of distress" (Obad 14).

In a just war, there is no gloating. According to Catholic theologian George Weigel, the peace that follows war "coexists with broken hearts and wounded souls. It is to be built in a world in which swords have not been beaten into plowshares, but remain swords: sheathed, but ready to be

---

1. Mary, "Catholic Teaching Concerning a Just War," § 2.
2. Mary, § 4.
3. Mary, § 4.

unsheathed in the defense of innocents."[4] When a time of war results in peace, there is no room for gloating, boasting, or rejoicing on the day of another person's ruin—instead, participants live with "broken hearts and wounded souls." We continue to live in a world in which there is hostility between neighbors, and we need standards for managing conflict.

This passage from the book of Obadiah is one of the Bible's greatest hits because it tells us that God will always judge nations that wage wars in a manner that tolerates gloating, looting, and the mistreatment of innocent people. Fighting often brings out the worst in people, but warfare does not require barbarity. Human rights must be protected, according to Obadiah, even in the middle of armed conflict.

Questions:

1. When is gloating, looting, and mistreatment of innocent people tolerated today?
2. In your opinion, is war ever just? What conditions must be satisfied?
3. In today's global war on terrorism, what particular challenges arise?

---

4. Weigel, "Moral Clarity in a Time of War," § 7.

32

Jonah 3:1–10

THE BOOK OF JONAH is a fish story, the only book among the twelve Minor Prophets that is presented in narrative form, but it is also much more. Although the prophet Jonah is best known for being swallowed by a large sea creature and spit onto land, the central message of the book is repentance. The book begins when God gives an order to Jonah, the son of Amittai: "Go at once to Nineveh, that great city, and cry out against it; for their wickedness has come up before me" (Jonah 1:2). This was a tough assignment for Jonah, a seemingly impossible mission. The prophet was being sent to the capital of Assyria, a powerful enemy of Israel, and was being asked to preach against it. So Jonah bolted in the *opposite* direction, taking off for Tarshish in an effort to escape the presence of the Lord. He hopped on a boat, encountered a storm, was thrown overboard, and was swallowed by the famous fish.

Can we blame Jonah? Being a prophet to Nineveh was a dangerous job, on par with being a timber cutter today. According to the Bureau of Labor Statistics, lumberjack ranks as the most dangerous job in America, with an annual fatality rate of about ninety-eight deaths per 100,000 workers. But timber cutters are only part of the story. Deaths also occur in significant numbers among fishers, pilots, roofers, trash collectors, truckers, farmers, steel workers, and first-line supervisors of construction and groundskeeping workers. In 2018, there were 5,250 workplace deaths, a slight increase from 2017.[1] There are at least thirty verses in the Bible about the killing of prophets, and Jonah knew the danger. That's why he fled from the presence

1. Braverman, "The 10 most dangerous jobs in America," § 1.

Jonah 3:1–10

of the Lord and ended up in the belly of the fish, where he spent three days and three nights, offering a prayer that ended with the words, "Deliverance belong to the Lord!" (Jonah 2:9). Jonah was spewed out on dry land, and then God said again, "Get up, go to Nineveh, that great city, and proclaim to it the message that I tell you" (Jonah 3:2).

After hearing God's command a second time, Jonah repented—he changed course and went to Nineveh. Still smelling fishy from his three days in a sea creature, he entered the dangerous city and walked for a day through just a third of it. "Forty days more, and Nineveh shall be overthrown!" he shouted (Jonah 3:4). This stinking, sticky prophet cried out against the city's 120,000 residents, not knowing if they would hear him, heed him, or tear him to pieces. To his surprise, the Ninevites believed in God and repented of their sins. Even the king of Nineveh rose from his throne, removed his robe, covered himself in sackcloth, and sat in ashes. He called everyone in the city to "turn from their evil ways and from the violence that [was] in their hands" (Jonah 3:8). When God saw "how they turned from their evil ways" (Jonah 3:10), God changed course. Instead of overthrowing them, God let them live.

So what is the message of the Book of Jonah for us? It has nothing to do with surviving for three days in the belly of a fish. Instead, it teaches us about how to repent, which means to turn ourselves around and serve a God of overflowing grace. We learn from Jonah about the danger of focusing on our own agenda and having pre-conceived notions about how God is *supposed* to function and operate in the world. Instead, when we reverse course and become obedient to God—even after a time of running in the opposite direction, as Jonah did—we find that our efforts result in life, not death. Obedience to God can open up new possibilities for renewal and regeneration.

The problem with obedience is that it is a tough sell. You hear the words "be obedient," and it sounds as if you are being asked to eat your vegetables and exercise thirty minutes a day. There's just nothing exciting about it—nothing to get you pumped up and inspired. In addition, obedience to God can be difficult because it challenges us to put the interests of others ahead of our own, turn the other cheek, love our enemies, pray for those who persecute us, and pick up our cross and follow Jesus. When we say yes to God's commands, we don't know where God will send us or what God will ask of us.

But notice what happened when Jonah turned himself around and practiced obedience. The "people of Nineveh believed God," the king called for the people to turn aside from their violence and evil ways, and "God changed his mind about the calamity that he had said he would bring upon them" (Jonah 3:5, 10). Jonah didn't get it right the first time, but he took advantage of his second chance and changed the fate of a great city. This passage is one of the Bible's greatest hits because it shows us that Jonah's willingness to obey God and proclaim a message to Nineveh resulted in new life for himself, and for the people and animals of Nineveh as well. When we follow Jonah's path, we discover that obedience leads to renewal instead of wreckage, enrichment instead of exhaustion, and life instead of death. The first step is always repentance, turning ourselves around and walking in the way of God.

Questions:

1. When have you tried to evade a difficult challenge, and what happened?
2. What is the biggest barrier to repentance? How can it be overcome?
3. How do you respond to the call to be obedient?

33

Micah 5:2-5

THE BOOK OF MICAH, named for a prophet from Moresheth in the land of Judah, begins with prophecies of doom directed toward Israel and Judah. Because the leaders of the people "abhor justice and pervert all equity," Micah says that "Jerusalem shall become a heap of ruins" (Mic 3:9, 12). But the book also promises restoration, and the fifth chapter speaks of a shepherd-king who will come forth to rule Judah. Micah anticipates a new ruler from the little town of Bethlehem, a rural savior who is not a part of the wealthy Jerusalem establishment. "Micah accents the rapacious economic practices of the landed community that exploits the vulnerable," notes Walter Brueggemann—landowners who violate the will of God "for economic justice in the community."[1]

But what is the particular significance of Bethlehem, described by Micah as "one of the little clans of Judah" (Mic 5:2)? In short, it is a "thin place," where the reality of heaven comes very close to earth. In *The New York Times*, writer Eric Weiner recalls the Celtic saying that heaven and earth are only three feet apart, "but in thin places that distance is even shorter." A thin place is a "locale where the distance between heaven and earth collapses and we're able to catch glimpses of the divine."[2] Off the west coast of Scotland is a thin place called the Isle of Iona, settled by St. Columba in the year 563. This rugged and rocky island became the cradle of Christianity in Scotland, and a Celtic Christian community has existed there ever since. On this island, the power of God is felt in the wind, like the "wind from

1. Brueggemann, *An Introduction to the Old Testament*, 234-36.r
2. Weiner, "Where Heaven and Earth Come Closer," 10.

God" that swept over the face of the waters on the first day of creation (Gen 1:2). The rough water around the island brings to mind the destruction of the Egyptians in the Red Sea and the rebirth that comes through baptism. A visit to Iona puts you in touch with the elemental and the eternal.

In similar manner, the little town of Bethlehem is a thin place. Micah says: "But you, O Bethlehem of Ephrathah, who are one of the little clans of Judah, from you shall come forth for me one who is to rule in Israel, whose origin is from of old, from ancient days" (Mic 5:2). Bethlehem is a small place, like the rocky Isle of Iona. It is the home of David, the greatest of the kings of Israel. And it is, of course, the biblical birthplace of Jesus. Two questions appeared on the cover of *Newsweek* magazine before Christmas one year: "Who was Jesus?" and "Why Bethlehem?" Inside the magazine, New Testament scholar Bart Ehrman explored the historical truth of the early life of Jesus. He wrote that the story of the Christ-child "can be founded not on what really did happen, but on what really does happen."[3] Specifically, what really *does happen* in the lives of those who believe that the Christmas story conveys a greater truth? What really *does happen* when we see Bethlehem as a thin place, with very little distance between heaven and earth?

Bethlehem is a place where we can experience the eternal and see God at work in the world. Ruth was a Moabite woman in Bethlehem who became the ancestor of King David. He was "a man after [God's] own heart" (1 Sam 13:14), a person who was as flawed as any of us, but who had a passion for God. David became the ancestor of Jesus, the one who brings heaven and earth together. His "origin is from old, from ancient days" (Mic 5:2), like the rocks of the Isle of Iona. Jesus was born in a thin place where God's activity becomes visible, where we can catch a glimpse of the divine. "How silently, how silently, the wondrous gift is given!" says the Christmas carol "O Little Town of Bethlehem," so "God imparts to human hearts, the blessings of his heaven."

Another truth of Bethlehem is that Jesus comes to rule with a unique kind of strength. He is "one who is to rule in Israel," says Micah. "He shall stand and feed his flock in the strength of the Lord" (Mic 5:2, 4). Jesus is a king who rules like a good shepherd, keeping his flock well-fed and secure. Coming from Bethlehem, which means "house of bread," he nourishes us with his teachings, his example, and his gifts of forgiveness and new life. Bethlehem also teaches us that Jesus "shall be great to the ends of the earth;

---

3. Ehrman, "The Myths of Jesus," 24–28.

Micah 5:2–5

and he shall be the one of peace" (Mic 5:4–5). Jesus shall be great, but he achieves this not by being a political leader or a conquering general. Instead, Jesus is "the one of peace," the one who continues to challenge us, in the words of Micah, to "do justice, and to love kindness, and to walk humbly with [our] God" (Mic 6:8).

Bethlehem is a thin place where heaven and earth come together. Jesus enters human life in this particular spot to show us that God is at work in the world. He reveals the kind of God we serve, and then grows up to rule with peace, justice, kindness, and humility. This passage from Micah is one of the Bible's greatest hits because it reveals that the barrier between heaven and earth is really very thin, in the place called Bethlehem and the person named Jesus. The town whose name means "house of bread" is a fitting birthplace for Jesus, the one who is "the bread of life" (John 6:35).

Questions:

1. What is a "thin place" in your life, where heaven and earth come together?
2. When you think of Bethlehem, what important images come to mind?
3. Where are the distinctive strengths of a leader who is a shepherd-king?

34

Nahum 1:1–11

NAHUM IS JUST THREE chapters in length, and the first describes the LORD as "avenging and wrathful" (Nah 1:2). The second and third chapters focus on Nineveh, the capital city of Assyria, and Nahum predicts the destruction of this "city of bloodshed" (Nah 3:1). The first verse of the book identifies it as "an oracle concerning Nineveh" (Nah 1:1)—the word oracle comes from the Latin *orare*, "to speak," and describes a word from God delivered by a prophet. "This particular connection makes the poetry of Nahum into a celebration of the fall of Nineveh," says Walter Brueggemann. Since Assyrian military power was uncommonly harsh and brutal, "the undoing of the empire and the fall of its capital city of Nineveh must have evoked great relief and joy."[1]

The "LORD takes vengeance on his adversaries," says Nahum. "The LORD is slow to anger but great in power, and the LORD will by no means clear the guilty" (Nah 1:2–3). Here, the character of God is "announced as the one who seek vengeance," observes Brueggemann, "and who will 'make a full end' to those who resist [God's] sovereignty." God's vengeance is not arbitrary violence, but "an imposition of divine sovereignty on a recalcitrant subject."[2] The power of God is seen in nature, when "the mountains quake before him, and the hills melt; the earth heaves before him, the world and all who live in it" (Nah 1:5). Nahum sees God as sovereign, the supreme ruler of all that exists—the God who is, in the title of a contemporary praise song, an "Awesome God."

1. Brueggemann, *An Introduction to the Old Testament*, 238.
2. Brueggemann, 238.

Nahum 1:1-11

"Who can stand before [God's] indignation?" asks Nahum. "Who can endure the heat of his anger? His wrath is poured out like fire" (Nah 1:6). "There is something deeply appealing about a vision of a retributive God who finally comes to set things right," says professor of religion Francisco García-Treto, "to subdue the unruly powers, and to establish sovereign rule over the nations. There is great comfort in the conviction that evil will be brought to a final reckoning."[3] Nahum knows, however, that the sovereign God is not all anger and wrath. "The LORD is good," says the prophet, "a stronghold in a day of trouble; he protects those who take refuge in him, even in a rushing flood" (Nah 1:7-8). The anger and wrath of God is directed specifically toward those who have oppressed the people of Israel, and Nahum says that God "will make an end" to Nineveh; "like drunkards they are drunk; they are consumed like dry straw" (Nah 1:9-10). He believes that it is ultimately impossible to oppose God or to frustrate God's plans.

Overall, the book of Nahum focuses on two qualities of God that are often misunderstood: Vengeance and wrath. If used to describe the emotions of God, these words make God sound demonic. But if they are applied to God's work of justice, they can be seen in a positive light. In biblical thought, "God's vengeance is an expression of his holiness," says David Ewert of the Mennonite Brethren Bible College. Typically "understood as God's way of redressing wrongs," vengeance is "directed at those who oppose him and who refuse to acknowledge his commands."[4] Vengeance is designed to turn wrong into right, and to advance God's work in the world.

Closely related to vengeance is the wrath of God, which is always directed toward injustice. When abolitionist Julia Ward Howe wrote "The Battle Hymn of the Republic" in 1861, she saw God's wrath at work in the Civil War: "Mine eyes have seen the glory of the coming of the Lord / He is trampling out the vintage where the grapes of wrath are stored / He hath loosed the fateful lightning of His terrible swift sword / His truth is marching on." Nahum requires that you see God's work from the perspective of an oppressed person, such as a slave during the Civil War. If you put yourself in the position of an enslaved person, then God's judgments make perfect sense and inspiration comes from words such as: "As [Christ] died to make men holy, let us die to make men free, / While God is marching on."[5] Since the people of Israel had suffered oppression, the wrath of God was

---

3. García-Treto, "The Book of Nahum," 603.
4. Ewert, "Vengeance," 788.
5. Brinton and Yieh, *Revelation*, 49-50.

experienced by them as a welcome relief. For them, God's anger was a part of God's divine justice and the wrath of God could have positive results. From beginning to end, the Bible teaches us that God answers the cries of faithful people and saves them from destruction.

This passage from Nahum is one of the Bible's greatest hits because it reminds us that God is on the side of those who are victims of unjust people or institutions. The harsh words of Nahum are a warning to us that we should not turn into oppressors, because God punishes those who oppress the weak, the different, and the unpopular. "His wrath is poured out like fire," says Nahum, on those who oppress God's people (Nah 1:6). Throughout the Bible, God is judgmental of human power and pride, but supportive of those who trust in God and God's ways.

Questions:

1. Where do you see the sovereignty of God most clearly?
2. What are your reactions to passages that speak of God's wrath and vengeance?
3. How do you believe that God works for justice in the world?

35

Habakkuk 1:1–4; 2:1–4

MOST SCHOLARS PLACE THE book of Habakkuk near the time of the destruction of Jerusalem by the Chaldeans, also known as the Babylonians. This is based mostly on verse 1:6, which mentions God rousing the "Chaldeans" against the Israelites. Babylon had conquered Assyria a few decades earlier, and was now attacking neighbors such as Israel. Some might find it odd that the book of Habakkuk is called the "oracle that the prophet Habakkuk saw" (Hab 1:1), since English speakers tend to think that oracles are heard instead of seen. But the Hebrew word *hazah*, "saw," means "to have a vision" in the prophetic sense. This visual language continues when God says to Habakkuk, "Write the vision; make it plain on tablets, so that a runner may read it" (Hab 2:2).

The Book of Habakkuk begins with a dialogue between the prophet and God, with Habakkuk complaining, "O LORD, how long shall I cry for help . . . The wicked surround the righteous—therefore justice comes forth perverted" (Hab 1:2, 4). Then God responds, "Look at the proud! Their spirit is not right in them, but the righteous live by their faith" (Hab 2:4). Habakkuk's complaint raises the question of theodicy (from the Greek words for "god" and "justice"), asking why the wicked prosper at the expense of the righteous. In this case, "the wicked" could be outside invaders such as the Chaldeans, people who "surround the righteous" (Hab 1:4). The prophet is calling for God to assert divine sovereignty, along the lines of the words of Nahum, and God answers by calling for the righteous to trust God to work for a better future.

The Bible's Greatest Hits

The phrase "the righteous live by their faith" (Hab 2:4) has particular significance for Christians, since the verse is used by the apostle Paul in his argument about justification: "For in [the gospel] the righteousness of God is revealed through faith for faith; as it is written, 'the one who is righteous will live by faith'" (Rom 1:17). So, who are *the righteous*? In Habakkuk, the righteous are people such as Job, who was "blameless and upright" (Job 1:1). Such righteousness continued in New Testament people such as Dorcas, who was "devoted to good works and acts of charity" (Acts 9:36). Job and Dorcas were not *self*-righteous—holier-than-thou, self-satisfied, and smug. No, they were truly righteous, which means being in right relationships. And what does it mean to *live by faith*? In the Hebrew scriptures, Abram was the first to show faith in God. After God promised to give him an enormous group of descendants, "he believed the Lord; and the Lord reckoned it to him as righteousness" (Gen 15:6). Abram, whose name was changed to Abraham, was made right with God by his willingness to believe God. In the New Testament, the apostle Paul picks up on this and says, "Abraham believed God, and it was reckoned to him as righteousness" (Rom 4:3).

The Protestant Reformer Martin Luther made Paul's insight the center of his theology, one which asserted that we are saved by the grace of God through our faith in Jesus. Luther wanted to be a good and righteous person, so he confessed his sins frequently, often daily, and for as long as six hours at a time. But after confessing his sins, he would leave the church and remember other sins that he needed to confess. This frustrated him, and he realized that he could not become righteous by human effort alone. Then he read the line in Paul's letter to the Romans that says, "the one who is righteous will live by faith" (Rom 1:17)—a line based on Habakkuk 2:4. In a flash, Luther realized that he was not made righteous by his good efforts, but by his faith in Jesus Christ. "I felt myself to be reborn and to have gone through open doors into paradise," said Luther. "This passage of Paul became to me a gate to heaven." The Reformation began when Luther made this discovery about the role of faith in making us right with God. "If you have true faith that Christ is your Savior," he said, "then at once you have a gracious God, [and] you should see pure grace and overflowing love."[1] Luther was inspired to preach the gospel, a word which means "good news," because he saw that the gospel was "the power of God for salvation to everyone who has faith" (Rom 1:16).

---

1. Bainton, *Here I Stand*, 41–50.

Habakkuk 1:1–4; 2:1–4

The words of the prophet Habakkuk inspired both Paul and Martin Luther, and they can inspire us today. In the time of Habakkuk, the invasion of the Chaldeans was coming, and the present felt out of control. Similar distress was felt in the times of Paul and Luther, and in our time today. But through it all, God gives us "a vision for the appointed time; it speaks of the end, and does not lie" (Hab 2:3). Habakkuk's vision speaks of the importance of righteousness and faith, in every time and place and situation. It tells us that God is in control, and that proud and arrogant people will not triumph in the end. Habakkuk's message is that "the righteous live by their faith" (Hab 2:4), and that right relationships are based on trusting God. This is one of the Bible's greatest hits because it reminds us that we can be right with God and with the people around us when we live by faith.

Questions:

1. When have you seen evil people prosper and righteous people suffer?
2. Where do you see examples of right relationships today?
3. What does it mean to you to be righteous and live by faith?

36

Zephaniah 3:14–20

ZEPHANIAH WAS A PROPHET during the reign of King Josiah in the seventh century before Christ. The prophet announced God's judgment on Judah and Jerusalem, saying that God would cut off "the idolatrous priests" (Zeph 1:4), but he also predicted judgment on enemy nations, saying that "Moab shall become like Sodom and the Ammonites like Gomorrah" (Zeph 2:9). The short book ends with a song of joy, one that promises, "The LORD, your God, is in your midst, a warrior who gives victory; he will rejoice over you with gladness" (Zeph 3:17). The divine warrior says, "I will deal with all your oppressors at that time. And I will save the lame and gather the outcast" (Zeph 3:19). Then God promises, "I will bring you home" and "restore your fortunes" (Zeph 3:20).

At the heart of this good news is the promise that "The king of Israel, the LORD, is in your midst" (Zeph 3:15). Zephaniah wants the people to know that they will be living *coram Deo*—an ancient Latin phrase which means "in the presence of God." That is what most people seek when they attend a service of worship, and it is why most services include songs of praise, an assurance of forgiveness, a word of hope, and prayers for healing. In *coram Deo* worship, people come into God's presence so that they can be restored to wholeness and strengthened for service. The Book of Zephaniah is instructive to us because it contains these elements of worship.

Songs of Praise. "Sing aloud, O daughter Zion," says Zephaniah; "shout, O Israel! Rejoice and exult with all your heart" (Zeph 3:14). The first command of the prophet to the people of Israel is to come into God's presence

Zephaniah 3:14-20

and rejoice with song. Most *coram Deo* worship services begin with people singing their thankfulness and adoration.

Assurance of Forgiveness. When we stand in front of our perfect God, we are reminded of our imperfections, which is why worship moves quickly to a prayer of confession and assurance of forgiveness. "The LORD has taken away the judgments against you," says Zephaniah (Zeph 3:15). And because we, as Christians, believe that Jesus has taken our sins upon himself for all time, this assurance of forgiveness is eternal. "The LORD is in your midst," says the prophet, "you shall fear disaster no more" (Zeph 3:15). When we are living *coram Deo*, we know that our forgiveness is forever assured.

A Word of Hope. No worship service is complete without a word from the Lord, one that gives inspiration, such as, "The LORD, your God, is in your midst, a warrior who gives victory; he will rejoice over you with gladness, he will renew you in his love" (Zeph 3:17). At the heart of this verse is the promise that God is with us and that we will be *coram Deo*, in the presence of God. The prophet Isaiah delivers this same assurance when he says that a young woman "shall bear a son, and shall name him Immanuel" (Isa 7:14), which means "God is with us." This verse from Isaiah is later quoted by the angel who tells Joseph that Mary's child is from the Holy Spirit (Matt 1:20-23). All of these verses are words of hope that remind us that God is with us.

In my novel *City of Peace*, a pastor named Harley Camden read a scripture verse to his congregation after a very traumatic week in the small river town of Occoquan, Virginia. "Hear the words of scripture," he said. "'Galilee of the Gentiles—the people who sat in darkness have seen a great light.' Here in Occoquan, we have sat in darkness, but the promise of our faith is that God's light shines in the darkness." Pointing to the stained-glass window behind him, he said, "Look at the face of Jesus in our window. Such calm in the middle of a storm. Jesus says in today's scripture that 'the kingdom of heaven has come near.' I believe that; the kingdom of heaven has come near, right here in Occoquan. It isn't fully present, but it has come near." Harley felt a rush of affection for the people sitting in the well-worn old pews, and as he looked around he remembered the church's original name. It had been called Emanuel Baptist, and the name Emanuel meant "God is with us." He suddenly realized that God was truly with them.[1]

Prayers for Healing. The final element of worship in a *coram Deo* church is prayers for healing. "And I will save the lame and gather the outcast," says

---

1. Brinton, *City of Peace*, 231.

God through the prophet Zephaniah, "and I will change their shame into praise" (Zeph 3:19). When we come into the presence of God, we ask for healing because we believe that God desires our complete restoration. God wants us to be returned to fullness of life and strengthened for service. "I will make you renowned and praised among all the peoples of the earth, when I restore your fortunes before your eyes, says the Lord" (Zeph 3:20). This passage from Zephaniah is one of the Bible's greatest hits because it ends with a strong affirmation that God is with us and the future will be good for us. The prophet tells us that God is in our midst as "a warrior who gives victory" (Zeph 3:17), and because of this we can worship and live as people who are *coram Deo*, in the presence of God.

Questions:

1. What does it mean to you to be *coram Deo*, in the presence of God?
2. Which element of a worship service is most important to you, and why?
3. How is your life impacted by the promise that God is with you?

37

Haggai 1:14—2:9

THE PROPHET HAGGAI FOCUSES on the rebuilding of the temple after the exile in Babylon, and the book begins with God commanding the governor of Judah and the high priest to begin work on the structure. The project was a top priority since the temple was Israel's primary place of worship and sacrifice, and was the spot where God was believed to be present. Haggai says that "the LORD stirred up the spirit" of the governor, the high priest, and the remnant of the people of Israel, and "they came and worked on the house of the LORD" (Hag 1:14). God asked them, "Who is left among you that saw this house in its former glory? How does it look to you now? Is it not in your sight as nothing?" (Hag 2:3). At this point, the rebuilt temple was nothing more than a foundation.

In spite of this unimpressive sight, God tells the people and their leaders to "take courage ... for I am with you ... according to the promise that I made you when you came out of Egypt. My spirit abides among you; do not fear" (Hag 2:4–5). God promises to "fill this house with splendor" (Hag 2:7)—making it more glorious than the temple of Solomon—and "in this place I will give prosperity, says the LORD" (Hag 2:9). The word translated "prosperity" is *shalom,* which means peace, harmony, wholeness, and completeness. *Shalom* "includes restoration of health, cessation of hostilities, and enrichment of individual and community life, prosperity in the richest sense of the term," writes Old Testament professor W. Eugene March. God "not only assured the people that the Temple would be made splendid, but also that the ill health of the community, its economic weakness, its vulnerability, would be replaced by God's 'peace.'"[1]

So, what are the characteristics of a true house for God? According to Haggai, such a temple is a community project, one that involves both the people and their leaders. It is a place of peace, harmony, wholeness and completeness, one that continuously reminds us that God is with us. Such a structure is currently being built in Barcelona, Spain: the Sagrada Familia Church. The architect was Antoni Gaudi, and the innovative church is still under construction after more than 135 years, containing a mixture of Gothic and Art Nouveau elements. Gaudi labored over his church for forty-three years, giving his all to God—or at least to the Holy Family, which is what *Sagrada Familia* means in Spanish. The next step in the construction of Gaudi's church will be the completion of a 550-foot high "Tower of Jesus." It is scheduled to be finished by 2026, the 100th anniversary of Gaudi's death.

The Sagrada Familia Church seems to fulfill the promise made by God to Haggai, "I will fill this house with splendor" (Hag 2:7), and it joins the rebuilding of the temple in offering us guidance for our own places of worship. Such structures should be:

Community projects, involving both the people and their leaders. Haggai tells us that God stirred up the spirit of two leaders and "the spirit of all the remnant of the people" (Hag 1:14). "The response of all sectors of the community to Haggai's plea [was] immediate and unanimous," write biblical scholars Carol and Eric Meyers.[2] In Barcelona, Sagrada Familia was started by Gaudi, but it will be completed by members of the community. In similar manner, our houses of worship should involve the spirit, courage and efforts of a large number of people. Without the faith and commitment of a robust community, a church is just a building.

Places of peace, harmony, wholeness and completeness. "In this place I will give prosperity," says God, using the Hebrew word that also means peace, harmony, well-being, wholeness, and completeness (Hag 2:9). Sagrada Familia is full of shapes and images that reveal the glory of God in creation, and in a similar manner, our churches should be designed to offer us peace and harmony. Our time in worship should comfort us and challenge us, leaving us with feelings of well-being, wholeness, and completeness.

---

1. March, "The Book of Haggai," 725.
2. Meyers and Meyers, *The Anchor Bible*, 43.

Haggai 1:14—2:9

Reminders that God is with us. In Jerusalem, the temple was "the house of the LORD of hosts" (Hag 1:14). In Barcelona, Sagrada Familia is a community of faith that is building the "Tower of Jesus." Jesus is a sign that God is with us, the one who fulfills the prophecy of "Emmanuel," which means, "God is with us" (Matt 1:23). All churches should offer the sure sense that God is present and working for good in our lives.

Our places of worship are most valuable when they are built by the entire community of faith, offered in the service of something much bigger and more lasting than individual lives. Like the people of Jerusalem and Barcelona, we are to hold nothing back, but give ourselves fully to God. This passage from Haggai is one of the Bible's greatest hits because it reminds us that our churches are community projects, places of peace, and reminders that God is with us. When we build in this way, the words of God come true for us: "My spirit abides among you; do not fear" (Hag 2:5).

Questions:

1. What does the Hebrew word *shalom* mean to you?
2. Where do you find splendor in your house of worship?
3. How do you give yourself to God in your community of faith?

38

Zechariah 9:9–12

THE BOOK OF ZECHARIAH begins with a call for Israel to return to God, and contains visions ranging from "a man riding on a red horse" (Zech 1:8) to "four chariots coming out from between two mountains" (Zech 6:1). The prophet then proclaims judgment on Israel's enemies and predicts the coming ruler of God's people, one who will arrive in Jerusalem on a donkey. "Rejoice greatly, O daughter Zion!" says Zechariah. "Lo, your king comes to you; triumphant and victorious is he, humble and riding on a donkey" (Zech 9:9). In ancient times, leaders would ride donkeys in civil processions and horses in military ones, so a king arriving on a donkey would indicate that the person was arriving in peace. The book of 1 Kings speaks of Solomon riding a donkey when he was recognized as the new king of Israel (1 Kgs 1:33).

Zechariah proclaims the coming of a triumphant king, much as Matthew does when he describes the entry of the "Son of David" into Jerusalem (Matt 21:9). According to Zechariah, God's ruler will be a person of peace: "He will cut off the chariot from Ephraim . . . and he shall command peace to the nations" (Zech 9:10). God's messiah will be the Lord of all: "his dominion shall be from sea to sea, and from the River to the ends of the earth" (Zech 9:10). This king will also remind people of God's eternal covenant with them and be an agent of God's restoration: "As for you also, because of the blood of my covenant with you, I will set your prisoners free from the waterless pit. Return to your stronghold, O prisoners of hope; today I declare that I will restore to you double" (Zech 9:11–12). Because this particular ruler is the Lord of all, a sign of God's covenant, and an agent of

Zechariah 9:9–12

peace and restoration, most Christians associate him with Jesus. He is an apocalyptic king, one who is part of God's revelation to the world, ushering in the kingdom of God. But what about *the donkey* that this king rides into Jerusalem? Is there significance to this particular animal?

For many years, animals were thought of as cheap and disposable props on the movie sets of Hollywood. As films were being made, horses were shocked, tripped, and forced to run into trenches. Wires were strung around their ankles and then yanked by the rider to make the horse fall on cue. Six horses were killed during the filming of *Ben-Hur* in 1924, and twenty-five were killed or euthanized during *The Charge of the Light Brigade* in 1935. Then an organization called "American Humane" got into the act and opened a Hollywood office to enforce standards for the protection of animals. In the 1950s, they sponsored the first of an annual PATSY award ceremony. The "Performing Animal Top Star of the Year" is the Academy Award for animal actors. Francis the Mule was the first PATSY winner in 1951, and later winners included Roy Rogers' horse Trigger and Arnold the Pig from *Green Acres*.[1] If the PATSY award had been around in biblical times, the animal who carried Jesus certainly would have been the winner.

Matthew tells us that Jesus sends two of his disciples into the village of Bethphage to fetch a donkey and a colt. This is to fulfill what had been spoken by Zechariah, "Look, your king is coming to you," said the prophet, "humble, and mounted on a donkey, and on a colt, the foal of a donkey" (Matt 21:5, based on Zech 9:9). Jesus enters Jerusalem as Zechariah had predicted, and a large crowd spreads cloaks and branches on the road in front of him. They greet him as their king, shouting "Hosanna to the Son of David! Blessed is the one who comes in the name of the Lord!" (Matt 21:8–9).

Aside from Jesus the messianic king, the donkey is the hero of this story. This PATSY-winning animal carries Christ forward in ministry and mission, and that is what Christians are challenged to do as well. The donkey was a Christ-bearer, or a *Christopher* (derived from the Greek *Christos* combined with *pherein* "to bear, to carry"). Being a Christopher means letting love be genuine, hating what is evil, and holding fast to what is good. It involves rejoicing in hope, being patient in suffering, and persevering in prayer. To be a Christ-bearer means that we contribute to the needs of the saints, extend hospitality to strangers, and even go so far as to bless those who persecute us. It means that when our whole city is "in turmoil,"

---

1. Orlean, "Animal action," 92.

as Jerusalem was on Palm Sunday, and the people around us ask "Who is this?" (Matt 21:10), we'll be able to give them an answer that shows them the way to everlasting peace and salvation.

If we can pull this off, and model our lives on being a Christopher, we will discover the joy that comes from carrying Christ. We'll know the glory of hearing hosannas, the thrill of close contact with Jesus, the excitement of accepting a challenge, and the deep satisfaction of knowing that we are walking in the way of God. This passage from Zechariah is one of the Bible's greatest hits because it tells us about the animal who carried God's king into Jerusalem, and teaches us what it means to be a bearer of Jesus Christ in the world today.

Questions:

1. What is the significance of a king riding on a donkey?
2. Where do you see the hope of Zechariah fulfilled in Jesus?
3. How can you be a Christopher, a Christ-bearer, in your daily life?

39

Malachi 3:1–4

MALACHI IS THE LAST of the twelve Minor Prophets, and his book is the final entry in the Christian Old Testament. In Jewish Bibles, the Prophets section is followed by the Writings section, which usually ends with Chronicles. The name Malachi means "my messenger," and over the course of four chapters the prophet delivers messages about the improper sacrifices offered by Israel's priests, the abomination of marrying foreign women, the failure to bring full tithes to God, and a day of judgment in which God will send "the prophet Elijah before the great and terrible day of the LORD comes" (Mal 4:5). In the third chapter, God says through the prophet Malachi, "See, I am sending my messenger to prepare the way before me" (Mal 3:1). This messenger is coming to purify the priesthood, so that the offerings of Judah and Jerusalem will be acceptable once again. "But who can endure the day of his coming, and who can stand when he appears? For he is like a refiner's fire" (Mal 3:2).

This line from Malachi has been made famous by Handel's *Messiah*, in which a soloist sings, "But who may abide the day of His coming, and who shall stand when He appeareth? For He is like a refiner's fire." The messenger of God is presented as a fire that burns away impurities, and the music reinforces this powerful image. According to music scholar Judith Eckelmeyer, "The repeated 16th-note pattern in the accompaniment shimmers like glowing coals; then the pitches in the strings leap by octaves, like flames being fanned in a furnace. Downward runs by the singer suggest the dross melting away in the conflagration; then upward leaps spew flame and superheated gases."[1]

Handel's musical imagery is intense and vivid, and his artistry continues when the chorus sings the next line from the Book of Malachi: "And He shall purify the sons of Levi, that they may offer unto the Lord an offering in righteousness." At this point, the voices of the chorus "leap up to four repeated high eighth notes which occur on the words 'He shall puri—...' These four notes seem like short hammer strokes. When followed by the long runs of 16th notes on the final syllable of 'purify,' they suggest a shaping and further smelting of metal, continuing the idea of the refiner's furnace."[2] From beginning to end, the music sends a message of refinement and purification—actions that Malachi felt were needed in a time when priests were offering polluted food to God.

But who is the messenger who will do this refining and purifying work? Some say that it is Malachi himself, since his name means "my messenger." But it is unlikely that the prophet would speak of himself as someone who would do this work in the future, when God's final actions would be revealed. By the time that the Book of Malachi was finished, says religious studies professor Eileen Schuller, "at least one stream of Jewish tradition had already identified the messenger with the prophet Elijah and his promised return."[3] Since Scripture says that Elijah did not die, but ascended into heaven in a whirlwind (2 Kings 2:11), he was well-positioned to return to earth and do this important work. Later, Christians identified the unnamed messenger with John the Baptist (Matt 11:10), a prophetic figure who was sent to prepare the way for Jesus.

The Book of Malachi is a fitting end to the Old Testament, because the prophet offers a message of purification that ends in hope. The messenger "will sit as a refiner and purifier of silver, and he will purify the descendants of Levi and refine them like gold and silver, until they present offerings to the Lord in righteousness. Then the offering of Judah and Jerusalem will be pleasing to the Lord as in the days of old" (Mal 3:3–4). Malachi's message is not of future destruction, but of restoration. At the end of the purifying process is an offering that is no longer polluted, but is pleasing to God.

In addition, although the book ends with a vision of a day of judgment, God says that for those "who revere my name the sun of righteousness shall

---

1. Eckelmeyer, "On Hearing the 'Christmas' Portion of Handel's *Messiah*," 6.
2. Eckelmeyer, 6.
3. Schuller, "The Book of Malachi," 869.

rise, with healing in its wings" (Mal 4:2). God instructs the people of Israel to remember "the teaching of my servant Moses" and promises that "I will send you the prophet Elijah" (Mal 4:4–5). In this final section, Malachi pulls together the Law and the Prophets, two pillars of the message of the Hebrew Scriptures, and anticipates the appearance of Moses and Elijah on the mountaintop with Jesus in the Transfiguration. This passage from Malachi is one of the Bible's greatest hits because it concludes the Old Testament with a promise that we will be purified in ways that help us instead of hurt us, so that we can serve in ways that are pleasing to the Lord. The very last line of the book creates a bridge to the New Testament, saying that Elijah will change the hearts of people so that God "will not come and strike the land with a curse" (Mal 4:6). This sets the stage for John the Baptist, who turns people's hearts with "the spirit and power of Elijah" (Luke 1:17).

Questions:

1. How has God's message had a refining and purifying effect in your life?
2. Who are the messengers of God who mean the most to you, and why?
3. How does Malachi prepare you for the New Testament that follows?

40

Matthew 22:34–40

THE GOSPEL ACCORDING TO Matthew is the first book of the New Testament, and is the first of four accounts of the life, death, and resurrection of Jesus. Matthew is concerned with placing Jesus in the story of God's saving work, which began in Genesis and continued through the Hebrew Scriptures. The book begins with an "account of the genealogy of Jesus the Messiah, the son of David, the son of Abraham" (Matt 1:1), and ends with a story of the resurrected Jesus commissioning his disciples on a mountain and telling them to teach people to obey everything that he has commanded them (Matt 28:20). Matthew seems to be presenting Jesus as a second Moses, giving new laws and teachings to Israel and to the world.

So, what was the heart of this new message? In chapter 22, a group of Jewish leaders called the Pharisees were challenging Jesus. One of them—a lawyer—asked Jesus a question to test him: "Teacher, which commandment in the law is the greatest?" (Matt 22:36). Jesus could have said that all ten of the Ten Commandments were equally important. Or that the Book of Leviticus was the greatest expression of God's law. Or that the entire Torah, the first five books of the Hebrew Scriptures, contained the fullness of the commandments of God. It was a difficult question, because if Jesus named one, he would be accused of ignoring others. If he said they were all great, he would look weak for not answering the question.

But instead, Jesus gave a tweet-sized response: "'You shall love the Lord your God with all your heart, and with all your soul, and with all your mind.' This is the greatest and first commandment. And a second is like it: 'You shall love your neighbor as yourself'" (Matt 22: 37–39). Jesus

Matthew 22:34-40

may have been the first and most effective practitioner of the tweet, a post on the social media application Twitter. The challenge of a tweet is to say something funny or provocative or profound . . . in usually about thirty-three characters. Funny, such as, "Everyone says to follow your dreams, so I went back to bed." Provocative: "Every saint has a past and every sinner has a future!" Profound: "The two most important days in your life are the day you are born and the day you find out why."

In just a decade, the tweet has become a powerful form of communication, one that may now have more influence than essays, fiction, or poetry. "Like any other kind of literature," says James Poniewozik in *Time*, "Twitter [literature] has its strengths, rules and tropes. Twitter is pure voice."[1] But long before Twitter was invented, Jesus knew the power of short, pithy statements when he answered a tough question in just seventy-four characters: "You shall love the Lord your God. You shall love your neighbor as yourself." His response was not just the Greatest Commandment but the Greatest Tweet. On this powerful formulation, he said, "hang all the law and the prophets" (Matt 22:40).

Preaching professor David Lose says that "our Lord names his center" with this greatest of commandments. Jesus is tweeting "the center of his ministry, the center of his mission, the center of the kingdom he has been sent to proclaim and build." The center is *love*, an even shorter tweet of just four characters. "By naming his center, Jesus reveals something not only about himself, but also about God." Jesus is telling us that "God's law, finally and forever, is the law of love. It is that simple . . . and that difficult, because loving others means putting them first. It means sacrificing. It means being vulnerable to the needs of those around us."[2] For Jesus, along with God, the center is love.

The problem with tweeting is that it is very easy to do. You can put a message on Twitter without having to back it up. But if people are going to follow Jesus in lives of love, they are going to have to put their words into action. Through the last days of his earthly life, Jesus succeeded in putting his Greatest Tweet into action. Soon after offering the love commandment, he gathered his disciples, broke bread, and shared a cup. "Take, eat; this is my body," he said. "Drink from it, all of you; for this is my blood of the covenant, which is poured out for many for the forgiveness of sins" (Matt 26:26-28). He shared that meal—and himself—out of love. Then he was

---

1. Poniewozik, "Twitter Lit: A New Creative Outlet," §1.
2. Lose, "Homiletical Perspective: Matthew 22:34-40," 203-5.

arrested, flogged, and nailed to a cross, from which he cried out and died (Matt 27:50). Jesus gave his life, his body, and his blood—out of love.

When Jesus says, "You shall love the Lord your God. You shall love your neighbor as yourself," he is not just tweeting. No, he is giving us the center of who he is, and is backing it up with his own life. Jesus went to the cross filled with love—he loved the Lord his God, and he loved his neighbors as himself. He loved each of us enough to die for us. This passage is one of the Bible's greatest hits because it tells us that when it comes to love, Jesus is not a tweeter. He's a doer. And he invites us to do the very same.

Questions:

1. What is the power of a short, pithy statement over a long, detailed answer?
2. How do you understand love to be the center of both Jesus and God?
3. Where do you see people backing up love with action? Where do you?

41

Mark 16:1–8

MARK IS THE SHORTEST of the Gospels, and scholars believe that it was the first of the biblical accounts of the life, death, and resurrection of Jesus. Since most of the stories in Mark can also be found in Matthew and Luke, it was probably the foundation on which these other two books were built. The first eight chapters of Mark contain an account of the ministry of Jesus in Galilee, and the second eight tell of events at the end of his ministry, on the way to Jerusalem and in it, including his death and resurrection. The story of the resurrection in Mark ends rather abruptly in most versions, after an announcement of the news that Jesus "has been raised" (Mark 16:6). Unlike the other Gospels, there is no story of an appearance of Jesus to his followers.

The word gospel means "good news," and can be defined in a number of ways. The good news can be the entire story of the life, death, and resurrection of Jesus, which is why the first four books of the New Testament are called Gospels. It can be the good news that Jesus declared when he said, "The time is fulfilled, and the kingdom of God has come near; repent, and believe in the good news" (Mark 1:15). Or, since the story of Jesus might have been lost without the miracle of Easter morning, the good news can be understood as the announcement of the resurrection: When three women entered the tomb, a young man in a white robe said to them, "Do not be alarmed; you are looking for Jesus of Nazareth, who was crucified. He has been raised; he is not here" (Mark 16:6).

We need good news, now more than ever. When the coronavirus pandemic hit, fear and anxiety immediately swept across the country and around the world. But then a new YouTube channel called *Some Good News*, or *SGN*, was launched. Created by actor John Krasinski of *The Office* and *Jack Ryan* fame, the *SGN* program was an immediate hit, trending #1 on the Internet. Some of the good news featured by Krasinski included people showing support to health care workers from their apartments in cities around the world—clapping and cheering out their windows. He shared a story about a homeowner leaving a gift on the porch for a delivery driver, and another about a man who purchased one hundred lobsters in Maine to help a local fisherman. Krasinski talked to a teenager who returned home from her last chemotherapy treatment and was surprised by a group of friends welcoming her back, while maintaining a safe social distance. "I cried for a very long time after watching that, just pure joy," Krasinski told her.[1]

When Mary Magdalene, Mary the mother of James, and Salome headed to the tomb on Easter morning, they weren't expecting pure joy. They were bringing spices to anoint the body of Jesus, a dismal and depressing task, and as they walked in the early-morning light, they worried about how they would muscle the heavy stone away from the entrance to the tomb (Mark 16:1–3). They were surprised to see the stone rolled away—that was *Some Good News*—and when they entered the tomb, they spotted a young man, dressed in white, which alarmed them. The mystery man tried to calm them, and then announced that Jesus had been raised. That was some truly unexpected *Good News!* Then he said, "But go, tell his disciples and Peter that he is going ahead of you to Galilee; there you will see him, just as he told you" (Mark 16:7). The final piece of good news was that Jesus was going ahead of them and would be waiting for them in the future.

We can be grateful that the Bible reports the good news of the resurrection to us, because this story does not appear in any of the other publications of the day. None of the records of Jewish leaders or reports of Roman generals contain an account of Jesus rising from the dead. Easter is a day like any other in these records: Criminals were crucified, uprisings were squelched, and the iron fist of the *Pax Romana* kept everything under its heavy-handed control. But the Gospel of Mark contains the good news that Jesus is alive and is waiting for us in the future. That's a story too big to be overshadowed by reports of death, disaster, and conflict. When Jesus was raised, he actually succeeded in putting death to death. He smashed the status quo and turned the tables on those who saw violence and corruption

---

1. Alexander, "The Office's John Krasinski launched a YouTube channel," § 1.

as unchanging constants in the world that we live in. When Jesus left the empty tomb, all bets were off and all expectations shattered.

At the core of the Christian message is the gospel of Jesus Christ: The good news that Jesus is alive and leading us to a better future. This news was true when the women visited the empty tomb, and it is true today. Whether we are facing a time of grief, a period of personal pain, or an experience of hopelessness or desperation, we can look to a Lord who is alive and well and inviting us to follow him. This news, the good news of the empty tomb, trumps all the reports of death and destruction that tend to dominate our daily headlines. This passage from Mark is one of the Bible's greatest hits because it reports to us that Jesus has been raised, Jesus is ahead of us, and Jesus will lead us forward. This news is real, compelling, and positive—the greatest example of *Some Good News* ever reported.

Questions:

1. Which definition of "gospel" means the most to you, and why?
2. How does the resurrection of Jesus change the status quo?
3. What is the significance of Jesus waiting for us in the future?

42

Luke 4:14–21

THE GOSPEL ACCORDING TO Luke is part of a two-volume work, with the second book being the Acts of the Apostles. Luke mentions women more than the other Gospel-writers, and has special concern for people on the margins of society, including the sick and the poor. His Gospel frames "good news" in a very specific way in the inauguration of the ministry of Jesus: "The Spirit of the Lord is upon me," said Jesus, quoting the prophet Isaiah, "because he has anointed me to bring good news to the poor. He has sent me to proclaim release to the captives and recovery of sight to the blind, to let the oppressed go free, to proclaim the year of the Lord's favor" (Luke 4:18–19). For Luke, the ministry of Jesus was one that reversed expectations by directing attention to those who were usually overlooked: women, the poor, captives, the blind, and the oppressed.

Jesus focused attention on vulnerable people with the precision of the tech company Facebook, which has launched a feature called "Disaster Maps." According to *Fast Company* magazine, this feature gives disaster responders a better sense of what is called "situational awareness"—real-time data that shows where the most vulnerable people are located. As a calamity is unfolding, these maps can provide aid groups with data on where people are and what they are doing, helping first-responders know where to place resources and how to evacuate people. Already, Facebook has used Disaster Maps in more than a hundred crises, including hurricanes, wildfires, and a volcano eruption in Bali.[1]

---

1. Paynter, "Showing Rescuers Where They're Needed Most," 78.

Luke 4:14-21

In Luke, Jesus was "filled with the power of the Spirit" and returned to the region called Galilee, where he grew up. He was being tracked not by Facebook, but by the people of that area, and a report about him spread through the surrounding country. He began to teach in their synagogues and was "praised by everyone" (Luke 4:14–15). When he came to his hometown of Nazareth, he went to the synagogue on the sabbath day. He stood up to read the scroll of the prophet Isaiah, which was fitting since Jesus went on to quote Isaiah eight times during his ministry, more than any other prophet. From Isaiah 61 he read the passage which began, "The Spirit of the Lord is upon me." Then he rolled up the scroll, sat down, and the eyes of all were fixed on him. He said, "Today this scripture has been fulfilled in your hearing" (Luke 4:21). Jesus was saying that he was there to bring good news to the poor, release to the captives, and recovery of sight to the blind. His mission was to free the oppressed and proclaim the year of the Lord's favor.

Jesus came to Nazareth to create a Disaster Map, one that focused on the areas of greatest need and enabled him to help vulnerable people. First, he brought "good news to the poor . . . release to the captives" (Luke 4:18). For several decades after Fidel Castro's revolution, Cuba was officially an atheist state. But the Christian faith of the people could not be destroyed, and in a period of economic distress the Presbyterian Church began to grow. "We are helping give the message of hope, peace and reconciliation," said Cuban church leaders. "The people are coming to the churches to find in the Bible, and particularly in the Gospel of Jesus Christ, an answer to their deep spiritual and existential needs." People who are poor and captive can always be found by Jesus.[2]

Jesus also offers "recovery of sight to the blind" and helps the "oppressed go free" (Luke 4:18). We know from Luke that Jesus was a great healer. He went directly from the synagogue in Nazareth to the town of Capernaum, where he cleansed a man with an unclean spirit, healed the mother-in-law of Simon Peter, cleansed a leper, and healed a paralytic. Jesus wanted to eliminate any physical or spiritual condition that prevented people from enjoying fullness of life, so he always kept them at the center of his Disaster Map. Christ's work continues today whenever Christians practice medicine or provide counseling, and when people who struggle with addiction find recovery in twelve-step groups, whether they are addicted to alcohol, narcotics, or sex.

---

2. Lewis, "The Presbyterian-Reformed Church in Cuba (IPRC)," *Cuba Partners Network*, § 8.

Finally, Jesus proclaimed "the year of the Lord's favor" (Luke 4:19). This meant that all of his talk about good news, release, recovery, and freedom was coming true *in that moment*! He was not talking about good things in heaven, but was saying that God was showing his favor at that time. "Today this Scripture has been fulfilled"—not tomorrow (Luke 4:21). The year of the Lord's favor continues when Christians support drop-in centers for the homeless, and the Scripture is fulfilled when people of faith take a stand to free the oppressed by building affordable housing. In Nazareth, Jesus made a dynamic response to human need, showing deep concern for the most vulnerable people. This passage is one of the Bible's greatest hits because it shows that Jesus wants to bring good news to the poor, release to the captives, healing to the sick, and freedom to the oppressed. Whenever this is done, the words of the prophet Isaiah are fulfilled, and the present time becomes "the year of the Lord's favor" (Luke 4:19).

Questions:

1. What overlooked groups do you think Jesus would focus on today?
2. As a Christian, what actions do you take to bring freedom to the oppressed?
3. How is Scripture fulfilled now, and how is this the year of the Lord's favor?

43

John 3:14–21

THE GOSPEL OF JOHN begins by saying, "In the beginning was the Word, and the Word was with God, and the Word was God" (John 1:1), echoing both the creation story in Genesis 1 and the passage about Divine Wisdom in Proverbs 8. John's account of the life of Jesus stands apart from the preceding Gospels, and his first chapter says that "the Word became flesh and lived among us, and we have seen his glory, the glory as of a father's only son, full of grace and truth" (John 1:14). This Word is *logos* in the Greek of the New Testament, and here it means God's reason or plan. "From his fullness we have all received, grace upon grace," says John. "The law indeed was given through Moses; grace and truth came through Jesus Christ" (John 1:16–17). Jesus reveals God's reason, order, meaning, and plan for the universe, and shows us the face of God most clearly.

Two chapters later, the most famous verse in the Bible appears, one that Martin Luther called "the gospel in miniature"—John 3:16. In a nighttime meeting with a Pharisee named Nicodemus, Jesus says, "For God so loved the world that he gave his only Son, so that everyone who believes in him may not perish but may have eternal life" (John 3:16). Author Max Lucado calls this verse "an alphabet of grace, a table of contents to the Christian hope, each word a safe-deposit box of jewels."[1] New Testament scholar Gail O'Day says it is an invitation into a new life based on belief "that Jesus is the Son of God and that God loved the world so much that God gave the Son as

---

1. Lucado, *3:16: The Numbers of Hope*, 9.

a gift."[2] The verse is a truly precious gift, inviting people of every time and place to believe in Jesus and receive eternal life.

What is sometimes missed, however, is the element of sacrifice that is present in this gift. In the verses that precede John 3:16, Jesus says, "And just as Moses lifted up the serpent in the wilderness, so must the Son of Man be lifted up, that whoever believes in him may have eternal life" (John 3:14–15). The Bible's greatest hit in the Book of Numbers tells us that in order to save his people from the deadly venom of poisonous serpents, Moses lifts up a bronze serpent on a pole (Num 21:8–9). In similar fashion, to save all people from the sting of sin and death, Jesus allows himself to be lifted up on a cross. That's a real sacrifice, one that saves all who look up at him in faith. Jesus goes on to say that God made a sacrifice as well, offering Jesus as a gift: "For God so loved the world that he gave his only Son." Because of this divine sacrifice, everyone who believes in Jesus "may not perish but may have eternal life" (John 3:16).

Actions speak louder than words. That's why the death of Jesus on the cross and the gift of God's only Son continue to resonate so loudly after two thousand years. When Jesus was being "lifted up" he was not simply being elevated; he was sacrificing himself in accordance with his belief that "no one has greater love than this, to lay down one's life for one's friends" (John 15:13). Such self-giving love has inspired people and organizations through the years, including businesses that make sacrifices. According to the website of the Chick-fil-A restaurants, their founder made the decision to close on Sundays in 1946 so that he and his employees "could set aside one day to rest and worship if they choose." [3] That's a real sacrifice, in an economic sense.

In addition, the Gospel of John presents the good news that God offered Jesus to save the world, not to condemn it. "Indeed, God did not send the Son into the world to condemn the world, but in order that the world might be saved through him" (John 3:17). If our own sacrifices had to rise to the level of the sacrifice of Jesus, there would be little hope for us. But all God asks is that we put our trust in Jesus—that we believe in him, lean on him, and organize our lives around him. That's why Sierra Trading Post, a mail-order company for lovers of the outdoors, has a bold mission statement: "Our business ethics must be consistent with the faith of the owners in Jesus Christ." David Rupert of *The High Calling* reports that the Sierra

---

2. O'Day, "The Gospel of John," 555.
3. "Why we're closed on Sundays." *Chick-fil-A Website*, § 1.

president intends for the statement "to hold me accountable for upholding Jesus' injunction to treat others the way I want to be treated."[4]

That's how people of faith are supposed to do business, in harmony with the loving sacrifice of Jesus. They want to do what is true and "come to the light, so that it may be clearly seen that their deeds have been done in God" (John 3:21). This passage from John is one of the Bible's greatest hits because it reminds us that "God so loved the world that he gave his only Son," a Son who offered himself freely on the cross, so that everyone who believes in him "may have eternal life" (John 3:16). When we live in gratitude for these gifts and do our best to be accountable to the example of Jesus, we become people who can show the grace, truth, and love of God to the world.

Questions:

1. Why do you think John 3:16 qualifies as "the gospel in miniature"?
2. What is the significance of the sacrifices made by God and Jesus for you?
3. How do you try to be accountable to the example of Jesus in your life?

---

4. Rupert, "Gospel on the sly," § 3.

44

Acts 2:1–21

THE ACTS OF THE Apostles was written by Luke after he finished his Gospel, which reported "all that Jesus did and taught from the beginning" (Acts 1:1). The Book of Acts tells the story of the first Christ-followers, with a focus on the ministry and mission of the apostles, a group of leaders whose title means "messenger" or "one who is sent forth." The early chapters focus on Peter and the followers of Jesus in Jerusalem, while the middle and concluding chapters tell of Paul and his missionary journeys through the Mediterranean region. The book begins with the story of the ascension of Jesus and then tells of the coming of the Holy Spirit on the fiftieth day after Passover. "When the day of Pentecost had come," writes Luke, the apostles "were all together in one place. And suddenly from heaven there came a sound like the rush of a violent wind" (Acts 2:1–2). Once again, God's Spirit is described as a powerful wind, much like the "wind from God" that swept over the face of the waters on the first day of creation (Gen 1:2).

The first followers of Jesus needed this spiritual power as they faced opposition in Jerusalem and later in cities throughout the Roman Empire. The sound of wind "filled the entire house where they were sitting. Divided tongues, as of fire, appeared among them, and a tongue rested on each of them. All of them were filled with the Holy Spirit and began to speak in other languages, as the Spirit gave them ability" (Acts 2:2–4). The Holy Spirit came with the power of wind and fire, and suddenly the international crowd gathered in Jerusalem could understand what the apostles were saying, "because each one heard them speaking in the native language of each" (Acts 2:6).

Acts 2:1-21

But some members of the crowd sneered at the apostles and said, "They are filled with new wine" (Acts 2:13). They didn't want to hear the message, so they tried to write it off as drunken babbling. But Peter raised his voice and said, "Men of Judea and all who live in Jerusalem, let this be known to you . . . these are not drunk, as you suppose" (Acts 2:14–15). The Holy Spirit gave Peter courage to stand up to the skeptical crowd and speak boldly about what God was doing in the world, based on the prophecy of Joel that God would pour out the Spirit on all people, and then "everyone who calls on the name of the Lord shall be saved" (Acts 2:21). Peter and the apostles were energized not by electricity generated by wind farms or coal-fired power plants. No, their power came from the Holy Spirit, a force which enabled them to speak in diverse languages and offer a word of gospel hope.

Such spiritual power is needed today, if Christians are going to be part of a church that brings life, joy, and hope to the world. Peter told the crowd that God's Spirit was going to change their lives for the better: "Your sons and your daughters shall prophesy, and your young men shall see visions" (Acts 2:17). New visions are being seen by young Christian radicals such as Shane Claiborne, who writes, "Jesus says the kingdom is 'within us,' 'among us,' 'at hand,' and we are to pray that it comes 'on earth as in heaven.' No wonder the early Christian church was known as the Way. It was a way of life that stood in glaring contrast to the world. Of course, everyone was forewarned that that in this kingdom everything is backward and upside-down—the last are first and the first are last, the poor are blessed and the mighty are cast from their thrones."

Convinced that the Christian Way is a life-giving way, Shane and a group of friends moved into a small row house in a poor section of Philadelphia in 1997. Their vision was to love God, love people, and follow Jesus, and they began calling their little experiment the Simple Way. Since then, they have shared food with folks who need it and run a community store out of their house. They have reclaimed abandoned lots and planted gardens in the concrete jungle. They have rehabbed abandoned houses and made friends with people in prison and on death row. Shane and his friends have seen a vision of another way to live—the Christian way. It is inspired by the Holy Spirit and directed toward changing the world for the better.[1]

Men and women have been drawn to "the Way" (Acts 9:2) since the earliest days of the church. They have tapped into a source of power that

---

1. Claiborne, *Irresistible Revolution*, 117–24.

comes from beyond themselves: a power that is not found primarily in programs, policies, or institutions, but in the Holy Spirit of God. This Pentecost power is an energy source that can keep people burning with love for God and for the people around them, while radiating warmth and light to a cold, dark world. This passage from the Acts of the Apostles is one of the Bible's greatest hits because it tells us that the most awesome power for the improvement of the world comes from the Holy Spirit, and that this Spirit gives us both the courage and the ability to connect with people around us in life-giving ways.

Questions:

1. Where is there meaning in the connection between the Holy Spirit and wind?
2. What gifts does the Spirit give followers of Christ today?
3. How can Spirit-filled Christians change the world for the better?

45

Romans 4:1–25

THE APOSTLE PAUL'S LETTERS are the oldest Christian documents in the Bible, and all of them probably predate the Gospels. They are arranged from longest to shortest, Romans to Philemon, and they are letters written to churches and individuals—addressing a variety of theological and personal issues. Paul's letter to the Romans was written to a community he had never visited, and it contains a compelling definition of the gospel: "it is the power of God for salvation to everyone who has faith . . . For in it the righteousness of God is revealed through faith for faith; as it is written, 'The one who is righteous will live by faith'" (Rom 1:16–17). Having grown up a Jew, Paul knew this line from Habakkuk 2:4, and he used it as the foundation for his belief in the saving power of the gospel of Jesus Christ.

In the fourth chapter, Paul digs deeper into the power of faith by lifting up the example of Abraham, who "believed God, and it was reckoned to him as righteousness" (Rom 4:3). He knew that for thousands of years, the term "righteousness" had been associated with adhering to a moral code based in the law of God, as in "the righteous hate falsehood" (Prov 13:5) and "the thoughts of the righteous are just" (Prov 12:5). But Paul had come to see that "there is no one who is righteous, not even one" (Rom 3:10). Looking inward, he confessed, "I can will what is right, but I cannot do it. For I do not do the good I want, but the evil I do not want is what I do" (Rom 7:18–19).

Paul realized that there must be a better way to be justified or reckoned as righteous. And fortunately, he found it in faith. He asked the Romans, "What then are we to say was gained by Abraham, our ancestor according to the flesh? For if Abraham was justified by works, he has something to boast about, but not before God" (Rom 4:1–2). But instead of receiving credit for good works, "Abraham believed God, and it was reckoned to him as righteousness" (Rom 4:3, quoting Gen 15:6). Paul read the Book of Genesis and saw that it was Abraham's faith that made him righteous, not his works.

When Paul made this discovery, he reinvented the wheel. His insight was as fresh and unexpected as the invention of the Morph Wheel, a wheel that actually folds. According to *The Atlantic* magazine, a designer named Duncan Fitzsimmons began by wanting to invent a smaller foldable bicycle, and then he realized that disabled people would be helped by having wheelchairs that could collapse and become tiny. So Fitzsimmons invented Morph Wheels, which fold from twenty-four inches wide to about half that size. Made of glass-filled nylon, these wheels are narrow enough to fit in an airplane's overhead bin, and they can be attached to any wheelchair with a quick-release axle. This is the first major reinvention of the wheel in seven thousand years of history.[1]

In similar manner, Paul discovered that Abraham received God's promises through "the righteousness of faith" (Rom 4:13), after centuries of assuming that Abraham was "justified by works" (Rom 4:2). This insight meant that righteousness can be gained by all who "share the faith of Abraham" (Rom 4:16), even if they are not able to follow God's law to the letter. You might say that the cumbersome wheelchair of religious devotion collapsed and fit into the lives of all who have faith in Christ. "For we hold that a person is justified by faith apart from works prescribed by the law," said Paul to the Romans (Rom 3:28). This is made possible by the God who sent Jesus to make everything right, beginning with our relationship with God. As preaching professor Thomas Long writes, "Every paragraph of Romans is about how people are free to live, believe, and hope when they are confident that God's life-giving victory is sure."[2]

Faith is not about purity, devotion, and rigor. Instead, it is a willingness to trust Jesus and walk behind him on the path of life. Abraham put this kind of trust in God, and he "did not weaken in faith when he considered his own body, which was already as good as dead," said Paul, "or when he considered the barrenness of Sarah's womb" (Rom 4:19). Instead, Abraham trusted God to be the one "who gives life to the dead and calls into existence the things that do not exist" (Rom 4:17). And sure enough,

---

1. Smith, "Reinventing the wheel," 26.
2. Long, "Preaching Romans Today," 273.

God did what was promised, and made Abraham "the father of many nations" (Rom 4:17).

When we have this kind of faith, we are made right with God—both now and eternally. This passage from Romans is one of the Bible's greatest hits because it reinvents righteousness by showing that we are made right through our faith in Jesus Christ. This means that we can trust God to work through us, even when our bodies fail us. We can trust Jesus to lead us, even when we wander through a thicket of difficult moral choices. We can trust the Holy Spirit to uplift us, even when we disappoint ourselves and others. Being righteous in these situations does not come from moral perfection, but is based on being made right with God through our faith in Jesus.

Questions:

1. What do you see as the biggest challenge of living a righteous life?
2. How does faith justify us, making us right with God?
3. When do you find it most difficult to trust Jesus and God?

46

1 Corinthians 13:4–8

PAUL'S FIRST LETTER TO the Corinthians was written to followers of Jesus in the Greek city of Corinth, in response to a report that there were divisions in the church. "For it has been reported to me," wrote Paul, "that there are quarrels among you" (1 Cor 1:11). Paul reminded the Corinthians of the importance of the sacrifice of Christ (1 Cor 2:2), and encouraged the stronger members of the community to serve the weaker members (1 Cor 10:24). Using the image of the church as a body—the body of Christ—he told them that "God has so arranged the body, giving the greater honor to the inferior member, that there may be no dissension within the body, but the members may have the same care for one another" (1 Cor 12:24-25). Then he offered a powerful chapter on the meaning of love.

First Corinthians 13 is a biblical greatest hit in many wedding ceremonies today. According to the website *Forever Bride*, the top Scripture verses for weddings are, from third place to first: "Ephesians 5:22-33: *Wives, submit yourselves to your own husbands as you do to the Lord . . .* *WARNING* This verse often gets taken out of context. For more info, read all of Ephesians . . . Romans 12:10: *Be devoted to one another in love. Honor one another above yourselves.* This verse will demonstrate your level of commitment and investment to your partner . . . 1 Corinthians 13:4-8: *Love is patient, love is kind. It does not envy, it does not boast, it is not proud . . . Love never fails.* The Bible shares that love is more than a feeling. It is full of action."[1]

---

1. "The Most Popular Bible Verses for Weddings & What They Mean," *Forever Bride*, § 1.

1 Corinthians 13:4–8

While the apostle Paul was not writing specifically to wedding couples in Corinth, he certainly shared the perception of *Forever Bride* that love is more than a feeling that can easily shift or change. Instead, it is a decision, a choice, and a commitment to act in a particular way. The Greek word for love used in 1 Corinthians 13 is *agape*, which describes a universal, unconditional love that is not affected by circumstance. It is an unchanging love which begins and ends in God, as in the Gospel of John's greatest hit, "For God so loved the world that he gave his only Son" (John 3:16). God is committed to the choice to show *agape*, and as a result, God's love is always available to us.

So where can this love be found in the world today? The answer is not obvious. In a *Peanuts* comic strip, Charlie Brown says, "If I ever had to choose a way to die, I would like to die by poison. How about you, Linus?" His friend answers, "I would like to be killed by loving kindness." Charlie Brown says, "Yes, that would be a good way to die, but poison is much easier to get." Charlie Brown is right—it is not easy to get loving kindness, another term for *agape*. It is not advertised on television or in magazines, where the typical love is *eros*—a word that is better translated as "desire." We see a lot of *eros* in ads for jewelry, clothing, and luxury cars, but not much *agape*. Paul is convinced, however, that *agape* can be found in the community of people who follow Jesus.

"Love is patient," Paul said; "love is kind; love is not envious or boastful or arrogant or rude. It does not insist on its own way; it is not irritable or resentful" (1 Cor 13:4–5). Such love is grounded in the words and example of Jesus, who said to his followers at the Last Supper, "I give you a new commandment, that you love one another. Just as I have loved you, you also should love one another. By this everyone will know that you are my disciples, if you have love for one another" (John 13:34–35). "In seeking the good of the other, one finds one's own good," says New Testament professor J. Paul Sampley. "Love cannot be held; it cannot be seized; it is realized fully only in its being shared with someone else."[2] *Agape* is always a self-giving love, one that seeks first the welfare of the other person. This particular kind of love, seen so clearly in the life of Christ, "does not rejoice in wrongdoing, but rejoices in the truth" (1 Cor 13:6).

Paul goes on to say that love "bears all things, believes all things, hopes all things, endures all things. Love never ends" (1 Cor 13:7–8). Jesus spoke of the strength and sacrificial nature of this love when he said, "No one has

---

2. Sampley, "The First Letter to the Corinthians," 956.

greater love than this, to lay down one's life for one's friends" (John 15:13). New Testament professor Susan Grove Eastman points out that "like the cross of Christ itself, love may appear weak and foolish in human terms, but without it all language and all knowledge are powerless to do anything that lasts."[3] This love turns out to be the most enduring power in the world, and Paul predicts that "as for prophecies, they will come to an end; as for tongues, they will cease; as for knowledge, it will come to an end" (1 Cor 13:8). This passage is one of the Bible's greatest hits because it tells us that self-giving love begins with God, is revealed most clearly by Jesus Christ, and remains the central quality of a community that wants to live by the words and example of its Lord.

Questions:

1. How do you understand love to be a decision, a choice, and a commitment?
2. What are the qualities of the love that Jesus commands us to show one another?
3. Where do you see evidence that love is an enduring power in the world?

---

3. Eastman, "Love's Folly: Love and Knowledge in 1 Corinthians," 14.

47

2 Corinthians 5:16–21

PAUL'S SECOND LETTER TO the Corinthians was written after he became estranged from this community and feared that another visit would be painful (2 Cor 2:1). Although he wanted to visit Corinth, he felt that his leadership there was being questioned, and his ministry was being disrupted by people who were false apostles (2 Cor 11:13). If he came to the city, he feared that there would be "quarreling, jealousy, anger, selfishness, slander, gossip, conceit, and disorder" (2 Cor 12:20). He loved the Corinthians, and more than anything else wanted peace with them. So he made reconciliation the focus of his letter, saying: "All this is from God, who *reconciled* us to himself through Christ, and has given us the ministry of *reconciliation*; that is, in Christ God was *reconciling* the world to himself . . . and entrusting the message of *reconciliation* to us. . . . on behalf of Christ, *be reconciled* to God" (2 Cor 5:18–20, emphasis added). For Paul, reconciliation was the heart of the Christian faith—reconciliation of people to God, and people one to another.

But exactly *what is* reconciliation? In a sermon for the Duke Center for Reconciliation, New Testament scholar Richard Hays said that the interesting thing about the word "reconciliation" in ordinary Greek usage is that it is not typically a religious term. "Rather, it is a word drawn from the sphere of politics; it refers to dispute resolution. So one could speak of the diplomatic reconciliation of warring nations or, in the sphere of personal relationships, the reconciliation of an estranged husband and wife." The apostle Paul said that God "reconciled us to himself through Christ, and has given us the ministry of reconciliation" (2 Cor 5:18). God has worked through

Christ to resolve a dispute with us, repairing the relationship that had been broken by sin. The work of reconciliation has been started by God, and now Christians are challenged to offer a ministry of reconciliation, resolving disputes between individuals and communities. We do this, said Hays, using "practices that show unity, love, mercy, forgiveness, and a self-giving grace that the world could not even dream of apart from Christ."[1]

This is a message that the highly polarized and fractured Christian community in Corinth needed to hear, and that we need to hear as well. Today, we struggle with many of the same issues that afflicted the Corinthians: "problems of doctrine, discipline, and vision," according to professor of history Garry Wills, "problems of class, of gender, of personalities."[2] We need dispute resolution, and fortunately the work of reconciliation is being done today in churches around the world. In Berlin, Germany, a congregation called Reconciliation Parish sits right next to a fragment of the Berlin Wall that once divided both the city and members of this congregation. Since the fall of the wall, the congregation has worked to bring former enemies into dialogue, and they have found that reconciliation is often the result of people speaking open and honest words such as, "I am sorry. I acted in a wrong way." Overcoming alienation and establishing new and peaceful relationships is best done through conversation, confession, and forgiveness in a safe Christian community—one that is grounded in the reconciling work of God. Reconciliation begins with what God has done through Christ, establishing a "new creation" (2 Cor 5:17) in which Christ's love governs every perception and action.

At Saddleback Church in California, work is being done to resolve disputes between communities. Promoting reconciliation is at the top of pastor Rick Warren's agenda, so both he and his church members are trying to do this work in their community and around the world, as people who have been "reconciled to God" (2 Cor 5:20). Every year, members of Saddleback participate in a Christian-Muslim picnic, building bridges of relationship. They partner with African American and Hispanic churches in Southern California. In the African nation of Rwanda, teams from Saddleback have partnered with church leaders, equipped pastors, and worked on the issue of reconciliation.[3]

---

1. Hays, "The word of reconciliation," § 1.
2. Wills, *What Paul Meant*, 113.
3. Brinton, *The Welcoming Congregation*, 77–79.

2 Corinthians 5:16-21

Disputes need to be resolved in homes and communities around the world, between spouses, family members, friends, neighbors, church members, cultural groups, races, political parties, and religions. We are challenged to do the work of reconciliation today because we are hurting from division—as individuals, as a church, as a nation, and as a world. Fortunately, reconciliation happens when we speak open and honest words, leading to new and peaceful relationships. Disputes are resolved when we show each other love, mercy, and a self-giving grace. This work can be done in our personal relationships, among groups in our congregations, in our increasingly-diverse communities, and in the world around us. This passage is one of the Bible's greatest hits because it challenges us to be "ambassadors for Christ" (2 Cor 5:20) who carry forward the message of reconciliation, based on the work that God has done in Christ.

Questions:

1. How would you define reconciliation?
2. Where do you see dispute resolution being done well in churches today?
3. What can you do to build peaceful relationships in your family or community?

48

Galatians 3:23–29

IN HIS LETTER TO the Galatians, the apostle Paul was writing to churches in a region called Galatia, located in the central highlands of what is now Turkey. Having taken the gospel to them, he began his letter by saying that he was "astonished that you are so quickly deserting the one who called you in the grace of Christ and are turning to a different gospel" (Gal 1:6). The gospel he proclaimed was not of human origin, but was received "through a revelation of Jesus Christ" (Gal 1:12), and the heart of it was that "a person is justified not by works of the law but through faith in Jesus Christ" (Gal 2:16). For Greek-speaking Galatian converts to Christianity who wondered if they needed to add Jewish religious practices to their new faith in Jesus, this was a transformative insight. After receiving Paul's letter, they realized that there was "no longer Jew or Greek . . . slave or free . . . male and female." Instead, all were "one in Christ Jesus" (Gal 3:28).

The letter to the Galatians was world-changing, like a number of other letters through history. According to *The Atlantic* magazine, some of the most important letters of all time include Abraham Lincoln's five public letters that bolstered Northern morale and helped the Union to win the Civil War. "I am naturally anti-slavery," wrote Lincoln in the most famous of these letters. "If slavery is not wrong, nothing is wrong." In 1939, Albert Einstein sent a letter to President Roosevelt, suggesting that an atomic bomb was possible. Six years later, the United States dropped nuclear weapons on Hiroshima and Nagasaki. And in his "Letter from Birmingham Jail," the Rev. Dr. Martin Luther King Jr. called for nonviolent resistance to racism. It

Galatians 3:23-29

became the twentieth century's most influential essay on civil disobedience, and it inspired major civil-rights legislation.[1]

History was changed in significant ways by these letters by Lincoln, Einstein, and King, but it was totally transformed by Paul's letter to the Galatians. Before Paul put pen to papyrus, people were "imprisoned and guarded under the law" (Gal 3:23). The religious laws of the Bible restrained and protected people, preventing them from hurting themselves and others. "The law was our disciplinarian," said Paul (Gal 3:24), using a word that had a very specific meaning in the first-century Greco-Roman world, one that the Galatians would have known. The disciplinarian (Greek *paidagogos*) was a slave who supervised and guarded children, keeping them safe and overseeing their behavior.[2]

The protective custody of the disciplinarian was important but temporary, since the slave's services would no longer be needed once the children grew up. Paul said that we were guarded under the law "until faith would be revealed" (Gal 3:23)—in particular, until the faith *of Jesus Christ* would be revealed. People certainly had faith in God for many centuries, but history changed when Christ faithfully died and rose to new life. The "law was our disciplinarian until Christ came," wrote Paul, "so that we might be justified by faith" (Gal 3:24). Once Christ came, there was no more disciplinarian and no more requirement for being justified—being made right with God—except faith. The *faith of Christ* is important, because it is Christ's faithful death and resurrection that bring God's love into the center of human life. But *our own faith* has a role to play as well, as we say yes to what God has done by putting our trust in Jesus. Now that "faith has come"—Christ's faith *and* our faith—"we are no longer subject to a disciplinarian" (Gal 3:25).

So what is the result of being justified by faith? For Paul, it meant that all followers of Christ are now "children of God" (Gal 3:26). Until he wrote to the Galatians, the term "children of God" had been reserved for God's chosen people, the Jews, and it naturally applied also to the first Jewish followers of Jesus. But now, "in Christ Jesus you are all children of God through faith" (Gal 3:26): the circumcised as well as the uncircumcised, the keepers of the law as well as those who know nothing of the law, the Jews as well as the Greeks—all are children of God through faith.

Paul's letter changed the world by giving us a new identity: baptized Christians who are clothed with Christ (Gal 3:27). Dressed in this way, we

---

1. "What was the most important letter in history?" *The Atlantic*, 104.
2. Hays, "The Letter to the Galatians," 269–79.

take on Christ's characteristics and try to present him to the world: showing his grace and love, speaking his truth, and serving others with his compassion. Clothed in this way, all of us "are one in Christ Jesus" (Gal 3:28). "God has destroyed the barriers that divide Gentile and Jew," says professor of New Testament Frank Matera, "slave and free, male and female, from each other."[3] This passage from Galatians is one of the Bible's greatest hits because it gives us a new identity as children of God, based on being one in Jesus and one in faith, regardless of background, condition, and gender. United in this way, we "belong to Christ" and "are Abraham's offspring, heirs according to the promise" (Gal 3:29).

Questions:

1. What does it mean to you to be justified—made right with God?
2. How is your faith influenced by the faith of Jesus Christ?
3. Where do you see signs of unity (or disunity) in the church today?

---

3. Matera, "Galatians in Perspective," 245.

49

Ephesians 4:25—5:14

LOCATED ON THE WEST coast of what is now Turkey, Ephesus was a Greek seaport city that existed for hundreds of years before being swallowed up by the Roman Empire. Under the rule of the Emperor Augustus, it grew into a prominent, prosperous, and powerful city, expanding through the first century until it reached a population of more than four hundred thousand people. Paul took the gospel to Ephesus and spoke boldly for three months, making a persuasive argument for the kingdom of God (Acts 19:8). Later, he wrote his letter to the Ephesians to remind them that "by grace you have been saved through faith" (Eph 2:8). Although they were Gentiles, they had been changed by their faith into "citizens with the saints and also members of the household of God" (Eph 2:19).

As Gentiles, the Christ-followers of Ephesus were like uncut diamonds with a value that was hard to determine. Today, rough diamonds are popular among wealthy trend-setters, people who crave whatever is new and different in the world of jewelry. The gems have a certain natural, earthy, organic appeal, and they are sometimes a bargain since they include stones which are not suitable for cutting. The biggest problem with these diamonds is that you cannot easily ascertain their worth. Faceted diamonds are priced based on cut, color, carat, and clarity—the "four Cs" of the Gemological Institute of America—but there are no industry standards for evaluating uncut diamonds.[1]

In similar manner, the Ephesians were uncut, at least in terms of circumcision. They were considered to be aliens from Israel, strangers to

1. Wu, "That's quite a rock," P1.

the covenant, without hope or God. "But now," Paul discovered, "in Christ Jesus you who once were far off have been brought near by the blood of Christ. For he is our peace; in his flesh he has made both groups into one and has broken down the dividing wall, that is, the hostility between us" (Eph 2:13–14). Although diamonds in the rough, the uncut Ephesians were able to come into relationship with God and with their Jewish brothers and sisters through Christ.

But since they were still natural, earthy, and organic, the Ephesians needed additional refining. So Paul laid out instructions for them: "Live as children of light" (Eph 5:8). He knew that in order to sparkle, shine, and transmit God's light, some cutting would be involved: putting away falsehood, giving up stealing, stripping away "all bitterness and wrath and anger and wrangling and slander, together with all malice" (Eph 4:31), turning away from fornication and greed, as well as "obscene, silly, and vulgar talk" (Eph 5:4). Paul wanted the Ephesians to remove the impurities that kept them from being brilliant and beautiful diamonds, able to receive and transmit the light of God. He wanted them to live "as children of light—for the fruit of the light is found in all that is good and right and true" (Eph 5:8–9).

So what steps were involved? "Try to find out what is pleasing to the Lord," said Paul (Eph 5:10), try to discover the best Christian behavior in the face of challenging real-life situations. The Greek word for "try to find out" is *dokimazo*, which also means "discern" or "test." It is an active verb, one which means to examine and put to the test, as you would test a team of oxen. In the parable of the great dinner, a guest says, "I have bought five yoke of oxen, and I am going to try them out" (Luke 14:19). *Dokimazo*. This is not theoretical speculation, but it is down and dirty hard work—the same kind of effort you would put into cutting, polishing and shaping a gem. As you cut away what Paul calls "the unfruitful works of darkness" (Eph 5:11), you become ever more clear about what a Christian life looks like.

The goal of all this work is complete transparency to the light of God. In her book *Night on the Flint River*, Roberta Bondi sets out on a canoe trip near Atlanta, along with a colleague named Pam. They intend for the trip to last for the afternoon, but the outing quickly turns into a disaster—the water level is high, and the riverbed is littered with dead trees. They leave the river and begin to hike through a wilderness so dark that they cannot even see their own hands. Through this ordeal, Pam remains optimistic. Roberta writes that "Pam's love carved out for me a space in the wilderness in which it was safe to breathe." In Roberta's eyes, Pam is "completely transparent to God," so that for a little while she "can see God truly through that human being."[2]

In that dark night near the Flint River, the words of Paul to the Ephesians came true, "Sleeper, awake! Rise from the dead, and Christ will shine on you" (Eph 5:14). Pam became a brilliant gem, with the light of God shining through her beautifully polished compassion and patience. This is the goal of all our cutting and polishing—becoming transparent to the light of God. This passage from Ephesians is one of the Bible's greatest hits because it promises us that when we focus on what is good and right and true, we turn from dark, rough stones into clear, beautiful gems. As we try to find out what is pleasing to the Lord, we become a diamond through which the light of God can shine.

Questions:

1. Where is refining most needed among followers of Christ today?
2. What behavior do you think is most pleasing to the Lord?
3. How can you become more transparent to the light of God?

---

[2]. Montgomery-Fate, "The Memory of Wilderness," § 1.

50

Philippians 2:5–11

PAUL WAS A PRISONER when he wrote his letter to the Christ-followers of Philippi, a city in the district of Macedonia, located in what is now Greece. The letter is very personal, with Paul saying to his friends in Philippi that he longed for them with the compassion of Jesus (Phil 1:8). He had a desire to visit them again but did not know if it would be possible, so he urged them to "live your life in a manner worthy of the gospel of Christ" (Phil 1:27). Then he encouraged them to imitate the humility of Jesus, using a poetic passage that includes the Greek word *kenosis*, difficult to translate but often appearing in English as "emptied" (Phil 2:7). Paul understood this tough but captivating word to be at the heart of the Christian faith.

Of course, *kenosis* is not the only untranslatable word in the world. Think of the French word *frisson*, the strange intermingling of excitement and fear, or the German word *treppenwitz*, describing the witty response that comes into your head right after an encounter with someone. Then there are words from Eastern religions such as *Nirvana* or *Tao*—we have a sense of what they mean, but there are no perfect English translations. In the magazine *Scientific American*, Tim Lomas has written about the magic of untranslatable words and has compiled a list of over six hundred of them. He has discovered that exploring these foreign terms can make our own lives richer.[1] *Kenosis* is one of these words: It means "emptiness" but includes the deeper significance of the self-emptying that Christ performed on the cross. Jesus was "in the form of God" (Phil 2:6), said Paul, but he "didn't think so much of himself that he had to cling to the advantages of

---

1. Lomas, "The Magic of 'Untranslatable' Words," § 1.

that status no matter what" (*The Message*).² Instead, Jesus "emptied himself, taking the form of a slave, being born in human likeness. And being found in human form, he humbled himself and became obedient to the point of death—even death on a cross" (Phil 2:7–8). Jesus emptied himself out through *kenosis*, and the result was that God "highly exalted him and gave him the name that is above every name" (Phil 2:9).

Self-emptying resulted in exaltation. But how? For Jesus, *kenosis* led to glory and power because it was based on humility. He was in the form of God but "didn't think so much of himself" that he couldn't accept servanthood, an attitude of humility that we don't often see in leaders today. But President George Washington put effort into being humble, and it helped both him and our country. He was a general during the Revolutionary War, and after achieving victory, he laid down his sword—an unusual choice for a conquering general. Some people wanted to make him an American king, but he said no. After serving as president for two terms, he could have sought re-election for a third. Instead, writes David Bobb in his book *Humility*, "Washington opted to retire ... His ambition, above all else, was to act justly for the sake of others and his country."³

The self-emptying of Jesus was based on both humility and obedience. Instead of remaining in the safety and security of heaven, Jesus allowed himself to enter human life as a vulnerable baby. "If you want to get the hang of it," suggested C.S. Lewis in his book *Mere Christianity*, "think of how you would like to become a slug or a crab."⁴ Paul says that "he humbled himself and became obedient to the point of death" (Phil 2:8), and because of this choice, God exalted him. Christ's obedient self-emptying led to great fullness.

Most of us are not going to be asked to follow Jesus to the point of death on a cross, but we are challenged to show humility and obedience as we walk the path of Christ. Martin Hengel was a great New Testament historian at Tübingen University in Germany, a country in which professors are highly esteemed and put on a pedestal. But Hengel would often have his students come to his home on Friday evenings for meals and discussions. "He wasn't influential just because he was a brilliant scholar," says a pastor named John Dickson. "It was the fact that he let people come very close, that he shared his life with them—that humility is what made his influence

2. Peterson, *The Message*, 2136.
3. Bobb, *Humility*, 74–75.
4. Lewis, *Mere Christianity*, 180.

lasting."[5] Such a life of *kenosis* is in line with Jesus, who said that greatness comes from being a servant (Matt 20:26). Jesus himself came "not to be served but to serve" (Matt 20:28).

The good news is that this self-emptying does not lead to embarrassment and powerlessness, since "all who humble themselves will be exalted," according to Jesus (Matt 23:12), an elevation that was seen in the lives of people such as George Washington and Martin Hengel. This passage from Philippians is one of the Bible's greatest hits because it uses the word *kenosis* to teach us that the self-emptying of Jesus, grounded in humility and obedience, is the unexpected key to his heavenly fullness and is the promise of our fullness as well.

Questions:

1. What does the self-emptying of Christ on the cross mean to you?
2. Where do you see examples of humility and obedience around you?
3. How can you practice service to others, following the guidance of Jesus?

---

5. Dickson, "Great Humility," § 4.

51

Colossians 1:15–23

THE APOSTLE PAUL WROTE this letter to "the saints and faithful brothers and sisters in Christ in Colossae" (Col 1:2), a city near Ephesus in what is now Turkey. Paul was concerned about false teaching in their community, and wrote the Colossians to stress the supremacy of Christ as the greatest power in the universe. Far more than an influential religious teacher, Christ "is the image of the invisible God," said Paul, "the firstborn of all creation; for in him all things in heaven and on earth were created" (Col 1:15–16). As "the image of the invisible God," Jesus is the human face of our divine Lord. As "the firstborn of all creation," he joins the Wisdom of God as being created "at the beginning of [God's] work" (Prov 8:22). He is the Word of God through whom all things were created, "and without him not one thing came into being" (John 1:3).

Image of God. Firstborn of all creation. Creative power of God. The Christ described in this letter is not small and insignificant—meek and mild. Instead, he is a truly Colossal Christ! Paul's image of Christ in Colossians fits a medieval map of the world which has the head of Christ at the top of the world, his hands on either side, and his feet at the bottom. Jerusalem is his navel, with the new life of the resurrection depicted by a picture of Jesus leaving the empty tomb. The original map was twelve feet by twelve feet, painted on thirty goatskins sewn together in the thirteenth century. Called the "Ebstorf Map," it was found in a convent in northern Germany in 1843, but the original was destroyed during the World War

II bombing of Hanover in 1943. It was truly a Christian map of the world, because Christ covers the map and holds it all together.[1]

"All things have been created through him and for him," said Paul, sharing this medieval map's view of the world. Christ "himself is before all things, and in him all things hold together" (Col 1:16–17). Paul believed that nothing in all creation was beyond the powerful grasp of the eternal Son of God, and that he actually held all things together. This belief in the unifying power of Jesus was important in the first century, although it is overlooked by many Christians today. An exception is author Rob Bell, who says that the first Christians insisted that when you saw Jesus—a first-century Jewish rabbi—you were seeing God in flesh and blood. "Jesus, for these first Christians, was the ultimate exposing of what God has been up to all along." And exactly what was God's mission, as revealed in Jesus Christ? "Unity," says Bell. "Unity. To all things. God is putting the world back together, and God is doing this through Jesus."[2]

Such a statement fits very well with Paul's letter to the Colossians, which says that in Christ "all the fullness of God was pleased to dwell, and through him God was pleased to reconcile to himself all things, whether on earth or in heaven, by making peace through the blood of the cross" (Col 1:19–20). God uses Christ to reconcile to himself all things, in earth and heaven. Christ makes peace between people and God, and between people one to another. Christ is creating unity where there was once brokenness and separation. Through Christ, "God is putting the world back together," insists Bell.

So what does it mean for us to follow a unifying God and join the Colossians in serving a Colossal Christ? We begin by putting Jesus at the center of our world. In the Ebstorf Map, the geographical center of the world is the empty tomb of Jerusalem, with a picture of Jesus being raised to new life. Christ should be our center as well, as we try to live the resurrection in our homes, schools, and workplaces. This means forgiving others, as Christ has forgiven us. It means choosing life over death, as God did when he raised Jesus from the tomb. It means responding to evil with goodness, grace, and love. With Jesus at the center, we can begin to see that he is much bigger than the narrow world of our churches and denominations. Christ touches everything in the Christian map of the world, just as he does in the physical world. He is truly a Cosmic Christ!

1. "The Ebstorf Map," *This Week in Palestine*, § 1.
2. Bell, *Love Wins*, 147–49.

Colossians 1:15–23

After putting Christ at the center, we can be bold enough to join him in the work of reconciliation. This is the toughest of challenges today, because we live in a world that is racially fractured and politically polarized. But if we use a Christian map, we follow the God who "has given us the ministry of reconciliation" (2 Cor 5:18), another of the Bible's greatest hits. We open our churches for discussions, as Reconciliation Parish has done in Germany, bringing together former members of the secret police and their victims. We build bridges with outsiders, as California's Saddleback Church has done with its Christian-Muslim picnics. We organize interfaith dialogues about peacemaking in the Jewish, Christian, and Muslim traditions. This passage from Colossians is one of the Bible's greatest hits because it challenges us to follow a Christian map of the world and serve the Christ in whom "all things hold together" (Col 1:17). Colossians tells us that God wants to put the world back together, through both Jesus and us.

Questions:

1. In your experience, how does Jesus Christ hold all things together?
2. How does Christ create unity where there was once separation?
3. What can you do to move Christ closer to the center of your life?

52

1 Thessalonians 5:16–24

THE APOSTLE PAUL'S FIRST and second letters to the Thessalonians are possibly the earliest writings in the New Testament. Written to Greek followers of Christ in the port city of Thessalonica, Paul described how they should live a life that is pleasing to God, and presented the basic beliefs and common convictions of the first followers of Christ. He was determined to present timeless truths and to explain and defend the common ground of the Christian faith. Paul was not interested in creating a distinctively Thessalonian style of Christian; instead, he wanted to help people to be *Merely* Christian. He knew that such Christians would be "sound and blameless at the coming of our Lord Jesus Christ" (1 Thess 5:23).

Similar efforts have been made by a number of Christian writers since Paul, including C.S. Lewis in his book *Mere Christianity*. This book began as four sets of radio talks on basic Christianity, offered in England during the darkest days of the Second World War. Since then, the book's popularity has grown, and for many Christians *Mere Christianity* is their favorite religious book apart from the Bible. The book is a classic, says historian George Marsden in *The Wall Street Journal*, because Lewis "was determined to present only the timeless truths of Christianity rather than the latest theological or cultural fashions." The book is his attempt to explain and defend "the belief that has been common to nearly all Christians at all times."[1]

So what are the timeless truths that Paul presented? He began with a set of commands: "Rejoice always, pray without ceasing, give thanks in all circumstances" (1 Thess 5:16–18). Such orders might strike us as odd

---

1. Marsden, "'Mere Christianity' Still Gets a Global Amen," § 1.

1 Thessalonians 5:16-24

and out-of-touch with the painful realities of our lives—illnesses, breakups, failures, and job losses. We would understand if Paul said "rejoice often"... "pray regularly"... and "give thanks whenever good things happen." But instead he says that we are to rejoice, pray and give thanks *constantly*, without regard to the difficulties of our lives. Paul issued this command because he was focused much more on God and on Jesus than he was on himself. Rejoicing, praying, and giving thanks are important because they are "the will of God in Christ Jesus for you" (1 Thess 5:18). This focus on the way of God and Jesus motivated C.S. Lewis to write, "Give up yourself, and you will find your real self. Lose your life and you will save it. Submit to death, death of your ambitions and favorite wishes . . . and you will find eternal life."[2] As Jesus said, "Those who lose their life for my sake will find it" (Matt 10:39).

The next timeless truth, according to Paul: "Do not quench the Spirit. Do not despise the words of prophets, but test everything; hold fast to what is good; abstain from every form of evil" (1 Thess 5:19–22). A person who is Merely Christian is open to the power of the Spirit of God, blowing where it will and doing the work of transformation. In the magazine *Leadership Journal*, pastor and author Gordon MacDonald has written an article on "How to Spot a Transformed Christian." These folks don't look different from the general population, but they do have characteristics that are signs of inner changes. One of the most important is a passion for reconciliation. "They bring people together," writes MacDonald. "They hate war, violence, contentiousness, division caused by race, economics, gender, and ideology. They believe that being peaceable and making peace trumps all other efforts in one's lifetime." They take action in the community when they see "dividing walls that separate people, each of whom was made uniquely and loved by God."[3] Transformed Christians "do not despise the words of prophets" (1 Thess 5:20)—prophets such as Zechariah, who said, "render in your gates judgments that are true and make for peace" (Zech 8:16). Transformed Christians follow the apostle Paul in holding fast to what is good and abstaining from evil.

People who are Merely Christian tend to behave in a particular way. Instead of quenching the Spirit, they let it fill them and transform them. Rather than doing evil, they hold on to what is good. Listening to the prophets, they work for reconciliation and peace. All of this prepares them well for the second "coming of our Lord Jesus" (1 Thess 5:23), which

2. Lewis, *Mere Christianity*, 190.
3. MacDonald, "How to Spot a Transformed Christian," § 12.

most members of the community assumed would happen in their lifetime, because such an approach helps them to "hold fast to what is good" and abstain from evil (1 Thess 5:21–22). Best of all, they don't have to do this by themselves, because the God who calls them "is faithful, and he will do this" (1 Thess 5:24). This passage from 1 Thessalonians is one of the Bible's greatest hits because it describes how we can be Merely Christian with the help of God, Jesus, and the Holy Spirit. Such an approach to the faith can stand the test of time, because it is based on the beliefs that have been common to followers of Jesus since Paul wrote the very first of his letters.

Questions:

1. In your opinion, what are the timeless truths of Christianity?
2. What do you consider to be the marks of a transformed Christian?
3. How do you understand the second coming of Christ?

53

2 Thessalonians 2:1–17

THE APOSTLE PAUL WROTE his second letter to the Thessalonians to prepare them for the second coming of Christ, the day "when the Lord Jesus is revealed from heaven with his mighty angels in flaming fire, inflicting vengeance on those who do not know God" (2 Thess 1:7–8). As frightening as this sounds, Paul actually wanted the Christ-followers in Thessalonica to be *comforted* by his words and to realize that God is both just and loving. He promised that by practicing justice, God would "repay with affliction those who afflict you," and by showing love, God would "give relief to the afflicted as well as to us" (2 Thess 1:6–7). Paul knew that "the coming of our Lord Jesus Christ" (2 Thess 2:1) was more than a day of judgment, and that the threat of divine punishment could actually turn the Thessalonians into better people. In that sense, he was ahead of his time.

According to *The Washington Post*, a team of international researchers has discovered that people who believe in divine judgment tend to act less selfishly toward other people, and "they are more likely to adopt behaviors that can create and support large-scale cooperative institutions, such as trade and markets." To test this, the researchers set up experiments with almost six hundred people in six countries, from Christians to Buddhists to believers in ancestor worship. Each person played a pair of economic games in which they were given the chance to cheat or play fair. The researchers discovered that if a person rated their God as moralistic and punishing, they tended to be more fair—in fact, five times more fair than people who didn't think about God in this way. Concluded one researcher: "They're playing by the rules towards people they never interact with."[1]

Paul may have had a hunch about this when he wrote to the Thessalonians, but his intent was not simply to fill them with fear. In fact, he begged them "not to be quickly shaken in mind or alarmed, either by spirit or by word or by letter, as though from us, to the effect that the day of the Lord is already here" (2 Thess 2:2). He knew that there was a lot of doom and gloom being preached by people throughout the region, and he did not want the Thessalonians to panic. Paul spoke of the coming of a "lawless one" who would take his seat in the temple of God, causing all kinds of chaos. Don't worry about him—Jesus would destroy him (2 Thess 2:8). Instead, Paul wanted the Thessalonians to know that they had been chosen by God. While they should certainly respect the justice of God and treat each other fairly, they should also have complete confidence that God loved them and wanted to save them. The bottom line was this, according to Paul: *God is just and God is loving.* Holding the two together is a key to Christian life.

Paul did an impressive job of keeping justice and love in proper balance, while showing that divine judgment is intended to help us. Christians in the developing world tend to understand this better than we do. In his book *The New Faces of Christianity: Believing the Bible in the Global South*, Philip Jenkins writes that during decades of mass martyrdom, churches in Sudan read the Book of Revelation for its promise that God's justice would ultimately prevail. Latin American liberation theologians have seen their own story in biblical passages about divine judgment, as have Christians in South Africa who took stands against apartheid.[2]

Paul reminded the Thessalonians that *God is just,* and that divine judgment will correct all of the wrongs in the world. But he kept this message balanced with the assurance that *God is loving,* and that the Lord will save all those who are walking in the way of Jesus Christ. It is when we remember both of these important truths that we are able to be the people that God wants us to be: Men and women who play by the rules, act unselfishly, and cooperate with others. Paul assured the Thessalonians that they were on the right track. He described them as "brothers and sisters beloved by the Lord," and he told them that God chose them "as the first fruits for salvation through sanctification by the Spirit and through belief in the truth" (2 Thess 2:13). He encouraged them to "stand firm and hold

---

1. Chokshi, "Fear of a vengeful God may explain humanity's global expansion," § 1.
2. Jenkins, *The New Faces of Christianity*, 150–52.

2 Thessalonians 2:1-17

fast to the traditions that you were taught by us, either by word of mouth or by our letter" (2 Thess 2:15). And he closed by asking Jesus and God to comfort their hearts "and strengthen them in every good work and word" (2 Thess 2:17).

Paul's words are meant for us as well as for the Thessalonians. This passage is one of the Bible's greatest hits because it tells us that the justice of God needs to be always balanced by the love of God, a creative tension seen most clearly in Jesus Christ, our judge and our savior. As writer and minister Frederick Buechner has said so well, "The one who judges us most finally will be the one who loves us most fully."[3] Love and justice: When we keep them together, we are strong in every good word and work.

Questions:

1. What motivates you to believe in God's justice and treat other people fairly?
2. Why do you think divine judgment is a comfort to persecuted Christians?
3. How do you hold the justice of God and the love of God in balance?

---

3. Buechner, *The One Year Alive Devotions for Students*, 330.

54

1 Timothy 1:12–17

PAUL'S FIRST LETTER TO Timothy was written by the apostle to a younger colleague, one that he described as "my loyal child in the faith" (1 Tim 1:2). Paul began by admitting, "I was formerly a blasphemer, a persecutor, and a man of violence" (1 Tim 1:13). Paul was a blasphemer, convinced that he "ought to do many things against the name of Jesus"; Paul was also a persecutor, locking up many of the Christian saints in prison, and pursuing them "even to foreign cities"; and Paul was a man of violence, casting votes against Christians "when they were being condemned to death" (Acts 26:9–11). When Stephen was stoned for giving a statement of his Christian faith, Paul "approved of their killing him" (Acts 8:1). Soon after, Paul "was ravaging the church by entering house after house; dragging off both men and women" (Acts 8:3).

According to *The Atlantic* magazine, the worst leaders of all time include Jefferson Davis, the president of the Confederate States of America. Author Matthew Karp says, "He embraced America's deadliest conflict, over the right to own people as property, and by the end of it, he had earned the hatred of almost everyone involved." Also Nicholas II, the last emperor of Russia. According to Ahmad Alsaleh, Nicholas "took a reasonably functioning country and left it vulnerable to radical revolutionaries." In addition, the list includes Pol Pot, Idi Amin, and Adolf Hitler, men who were under a "diabolical influence," says Chris Cuomo of *CNN*. They gave in to the temptations of the evil power which is always "disconnecting people from the basic love of one another."[1]

---

1. "Who Is the Worst Leader of All Time?" *The Atlantic*, 100.

1 Timothy 1:12-17

The apostle Paul seemed to be a pretty awful leader as well—a blasphemer, a persecutor, and a man of violence. And yet, Paul told Timothy, "I received mercy because I had acted ignorantly in unbelief, and the grace of our Lord overflowed for me with the faith and love that are in Christ Jesus" (1 Tim 1:13-14). Paul was saved from being one of the worst leaders of all time by the unexpected mercy that God showed him. The grace of God was not doled out in small measures, but it absolutely "overflowed" for him. Divine mercy and grace allowed the apostle Paul to move from worst to first.

But what *is* grace, exactly? The Christian writer Philip Yancey was asked to give a definition of grace and he answered, "I don't even try." But he did tell a story. "I remember once getting stuck in Los Angeles traffic and arriving fifty-eight minutes late at the Hertz rental desk. I walked up in kind of a bad mood, put the keys down and said, 'How much do I owe?' The woman says, 'Nothing. You're all clear.' I said I was late and she smiled, 'Yes, but there's a one-hour grace period.' So I asked, 'Oh really, what is grace?' And she said, 'I don't know . . . I guess what it means is that even though you're supposed to pay, you don't have to.'"[2] That's a pretty good definition of grace, isn't it? Paul was supposed to pay for being a blasphemer, a persecutor, and a man of violence, but he didn't have to. Instead, the grace of our Lord overflowed for him with the faith and love that are in Christ Jesus, and Paul went on to become a top church leader.

Grace doesn't make a lot of sense if people get off the hook and then return to their bad behavior. But more often than not, the opposite is true: People who receive mercy and grace are usually so grateful that they turn their lives around, and do everything they can to show grace and mercy to others. The best part about grace is that it is a central part of God's plan, and it is available to each of us. "The saying is sure," said Paul to Timothy, "that Christ Jesus came into the world to save sinners—of whom I am the foremost" (1 Tim 1:15). Jesus came into the world to save sinners—not just Paul, but every one of us. Each of us is supposed to pay for our sins, but we don't have to, because of Jesus. Each of us is let off the hook, because Christ Jesus came into the world to save us. All we have to do is trust in him, and let him move us up from worst to first.

Paul was grateful for this mercy and grace, and he responded by becoming one of the greatest leaders of the church. As he said to Timothy, "I am grateful to Christ Jesus our Lord, who has strengthened me, because he judged me faithful and appointed me to his service" (1 Tim 1:12). This

---

2. Yancey, "Grace," § 2.

former blasphemer, persecutor, and man of violence showed his gratitude by turning his life around and serving the Christians that he had hurt. A similar transformation can be experienced by us when we receive the grace of Jesus and discover that even though we're supposed to pay, we don't have to. This passage from 1 Timothy is one of the Bible's greatest hits because it assures us that the grace of our Lord overflows for us with the faith and love that are in Christ Jesus. Like the apostle Paul, we can become "an example to those who would come to believe in [Jesus] for eternal life" (1 Tim 1:16). That's a big shift, for sure: from worst to first. But it is possible for anyone who believes, because of the mercy and grace of Jesus Christ.

Questions:

1. What failures from your past are most in need of God's mercy?
2. How would you define grace, and when have you experienced it?
3. In what ways have you responded positively to God's mercy and grace?

55

2 Timothy 4:6–8, 16–18

PAUL BEGINS HIS SECOND letter to Timothy, his "beloved child" (2 Tim 1:2), by giving thanks for the young man's Christian faith, which came to him from his grandmother Lois and his mother Eunice. He reminds his younger colleague that "God did not give us a spirit of cowardice, but rather a spirit of power and of love and of self-discipline" (2 Tim 1:7). Near the end of the letter, Paul looks back over the course of his ministry and observes, "I have fought the good fight, I have finished the race, I have kept the faith" (2 Tim 4:7). Using the imagery of an athletic contest or race, Paul describes himself as one who has competed fairly and kept his solemn promise to put out his utmost effort. Coming close to the finish line, he squints into the future and says, "From now on there is reserved for me the crown of righteousness, which the Lord, the righteous judge, will give me on that day, and not only to me but also to all who have longed for his appearing" (2 Tim 4:8).

Paul looks forward to receiving "the crown of righteousness." Better than the crown of flowers that ancient Jews wore at feasts, and more coveted than the wreaths given to victorious Greeks at athletic contests, this prize is to be presented by the Lord Jesus on the day of judgment, on that day when he confers honors on all who have kept the faith and looked expectantly to his appearing. It is like a Nobel Peace Prize, based on a lifetime of righteous living, but in place of a check for nine million Swedish crowns is a single crown, the crown of righteousness.

But how do you qualify for such an award? In many ways, you run the same kind of race that the Nobel Peace Prize laureates have run. You fight the good fight and finish the race, as tough as it might be. You face challenges with a spirit of power, love, and self-discipline. Yes, the struggles of Christian living can be grueling, the obstacles can be daunting, and the suffering can be intense. Paul tells Timothy that initially "no one came to my support, but all deserted me. May it not be counted against them! But the Lord stood by me and gave me strength" (2 Tim 4:16–17). In times of vulnerability and isolation, we will discover, like Paul, that the Lord stands by us and gives us strength.

Mother Teresa of Calcutta, the winner of the Nobel Peace Prize in 1979, certainly discovered this to be true. She spent her life building homes for orphans, nursing homes for lepers, and hospices for the terminally ill—according to the Nobel website, she was a "saint in the gutter."[1] In her Nobel Peace Prize acceptance speech she said, "I am sure this award is going to bring an understanding love between the rich and the poor. [That] is why Jesus came to earth, to proclaim the good news to the poor. And through this award and through all of us gathered here together, we are wanting to proclaim the good news to the poor that God loves them, that we love them, that they are somebody to us, that they too have been created by the same loving hand of God, to love and to be loved."[2] She tried to love others as God loved her, and to serve the poor alongside members of the group she founded in India, the Missionaries of Charity.

Like the apostle Paul, Mother Teresa fought the good fight, finished the race, and kept the faith. She put love into action over the course of her life, and as a result she deserved the crown of righteousness, an award more eternal than the Nobel Peace Prize. But she did not work alone. Alongside many other Nobel laureates, Mother Teresa was part of a team. In 1999, the Nobel Peace Prize went to Doctors Without Borders, in 2013 it went to the Organization for the Prohibition of Chemical Weapons, and in 2020 it was given to the World Food Program. All these groups were made up of individuals who worked together to heal, protect, and feed the people of the world. In similar manner, we can labor together in the church to be missionaries of charity, people who try every day to make the world a better place by putting love into action.

Jesus wants us to show our love to the fullest and to demonstrate it to the very end of our lives. The world needs this kind of Christian love, now more than ever, and it includes what Mother Teresa called "an understanding love between the rich and the poor." In the United States, the

---

1. "Saint in the Gutter—and Saint in Heaven," *The Nobel Prize*, § 4.
2. "Mother Teresa—Acceptance Speech," *The Nobel Prize*, § 1.

rich are getting richer and the poor are getting poorer, and there is not much "understanding love" between the two. In the year 2015, according to the Economic Policy Institute, the top 1 percent of families took home an average of twenty-six times as much income as the bottom 99 percent.[3] As missionaries of charity, we can reach out to the poor with Christian love, offering them affection and assistance without judgment. This passage from 2 Timothy is one of the Bible's greatest hits because it challenges us to fight the good fight, to finish the race, and to keep the faith, so that we will receive the greatest of prizes: the crown of righteousness.

Questions:

1. How are you challenged to fight the good fight and finish the race?
2. What actions or attitudes are worthy of a crown of righteousness?
3. Where do you see Christians working together to put love into action?

---

3. Reinicke, "US income inequality continues to grow," § 1.

56

Titus 3:1–7

TITUS WAS AN ASSISTANT to the apostle Paul, and was described as a "loyal child in the faith" (Titus 1:4). Having departed, Paul wrote to him, "I left you behind in Crete for this reason, so that you should put in order what remained to be done" (Titus 1:5). He also instructed Titus to silence "rebellious people, idle talkers and deceivers" (Titus 1:10–11), and to teach sound Christian doctrine. Admitting that "we ourselves were once foolish, disobedient, led astray," Paul said that "when the goodness and loving kindness of God our Savior appeared, he saved us" (Titus 3:3–5). He expressed thanksgiving for the gift of the Holy Spirit, which God "poured out on us richly through Jesus Christ our Savior, so that, having been justified by his grace, we might become heirs according to the hope of eternal life" (Titus 3:6–7). Paul wanted to remind Titus of the valuable inheritance they would receive.

Across the United States, an enormous movement of money will occur in the next few decades. Trillions of dollars will move from the oldest generation of Americans to their children, grandchildren, and great-grandchildren. The problem is, many people are not prepared to manage an inheritance. Recent studies have found that many heirs quickly dispense with the wealth they have received. According to *Market Watch*, a third of people who received an inheritance had negative savings within two years. "The vast majority of people blew through it quickly," said Jay Zagorsky, an economist at The Ohio State University. Sadly, the story of many heirs is not rags to riches. It is rags to riches... to rags. They don't know how to handle an inheritance.[1]

1. O'Brien, "One in three Americans who get an inheritance blow it," § 1.

Titus 3:1-7

While a gift of money is always appreciated, Paul's letter to Titus speaks of another kind of wealth: an inheritance of eternal life (Titus 3:7). Jesus came to earth at Christmas to bring us salvation, a gift which God offers us "according to his mercy" (Titus 3:5). Unlike the gifts of Santa Claus, salvation isn't based on whether you've been naughty or nice. Instead, it is a gift of grace, from the "goodness and loving kindness of God our Savior" (Titus 3:4). Salvation is generated by the mercy of God, and is available to anyone who trusts in God's Son Jesus.

Across the United States, many people are struggling with debt and don't see any way to rise out of it. They are anxious for an inheritance that will lift their finances from the negative to the positive. In similar manner, many of us feel mired in sinful and self-destructive behaviors, and we don't know how to escape them. We find it impossible to live as Paul recommended to Titus: "to speak evil of no one, to avoid quarreling, to be gentle" (Titus 3:2). Our sins feel similar to a crushing financial burden, which is why many versions of The Lord's Prayer include the line, "Forgive us our debts, as we forgive our debtors." God's salvation is the help we need, designed to save us from our sins, forgive us our debts, and wipe our slate clean. God saves us from the endless struggles of this life, promising us an endless life in heaven. And God does this according to his mercy, not because of any works of righteousness that we have done. All we have to do is trust in God's Son Jesus, the one God sent to bring us forgiveness and new life.

One of the ways that we can better handle our inheritance from God is to remember our baptism, the sacrament which includes "the water of rebirth and renewal by the Holy Spirit" (Titus 3:5). We are much more likely to waste our spiritual inheritance if we forget that we are baptized children of God, eternally connected to our brother Jesus Christ. Remembering that we are forgiven, reborn, and renewed can help us to hold on to the precious gift of salvation that God has given us. The Reformer Martin Luther had a challenging and stressful life, and one of the ways that he pushed back against despair was to scribble on his desktop, "I am baptized." By remembering that he was baptized, he was able to recall *who* he was and even more importantly, *whose* he was. His baptism reminded him that he had been reborn and renewed, saved by grace through his faith in Jesus Christ. He knew, in the words of Paul, that God's Spirit is "poured out on us richly through Jesus Christ our Savior, so that, having been justified by his grace, we might become heirs according to the hope of eternal life" (Titus 3:6-7).

Baptism helped Martin Luther to handle his inheritance. It reminded him that God's Spirit had been poured out on him richly, gave him the assurance that he had been justified by grace, and marked him as an heir, according to the hope of eternal life. This passage from Titus is one of the Bible's greatest hits because it reminds us that we are heirs of God as well, challenged to handle our inheritance in a responsible way. We don't want to blow through it quickly, like so many recipients of financial windfalls today. Instead, we should continue to see the value of Jesus as we trust him to continue to give us forgiveness, rebirth, renewal, and eternal life.

Questions:

1. What kind of an inheritance would be most valuable to you?
2. How is sin a debt, and what can be done to eliminate it?
3. In what ways are you helped by remembering that you are baptized?

57

Philemon 1–21

Paul's letter to Philemon is his only surviving private letter, and it is a very personal message to a "dear friend and coworker" (Phlm 1) who is a slave-owner. In the letter, Paul encourages Philemon to forgive a runaway slave named Onesimus and to welcome him back—not as a piece of property, but as a brother in Christ. He wants Philemon to embrace the Christian faith ever more deeply, so that he will see his slave in a whole new light: "no longer as a slave but more than a slave, a beloved brother" (Phlm 16). "I pray that the sharing of your faith may become effective," writes Paul, "when you perceive all the good that we may do for Christ" (Phlm 6). In the original Greek of the New Testament, Paul prays that "the *koinonia* of your faith may become effective . . ." Koinonia means sharing, contribution, fellowship, spiritual communion.

Among the finalists in the 2018 Scripps National Spelling Bee was a fourteen-year-old from Texas named Karthik Nemmani. Although this was his first national spelling bee, he showed the poise of a veteran throughout the contest, spelling with little emotion. He was confronted with the following words, any one of which could have caused him to stumble: Miarolitic, cendre, ankyloglossia, and jagüey. Nemmani spelled them perfectly, each and every one. The final word was koinonia, meaning spiritual communion. Nemmani spelled it out: K-O-I-N-O-N-I-A. Confetti rained down and Nemmani smiled broadly. He had spelled koinonia correctly, and was declared champion of the bee.[1]

---

1. Wang, "Champion crowned at Scripps National Spelling Bee," § 1.

The Bible's Greatest Hits

Most of us would break out in a cold sweat if we had to spell koinonia on a national stage, and we might panic if we were asked to define it. But the term is worth exploring, since it is a Greek word that appears nineteen times in the New Testament. Critically important for Christians in the ancient world and today, it is often translated as sharing, contribution, or fellowship. No insignificant term, koinonia is something that we need to understand and implement in ministry and mission.

For starters, koinonia means *sharing.* Such sharing is experienced today when American Christians take part in short-term mission trips to countries in the developing world such as Guatemala and Honduras. There, Americans have a shared experience of the Christian faith with their foreign partners, and they discover the power of faith, hope, and love in very impoverished environments. Lives can be changed through such sharing of Christian faith, especially when the experience is grounded in good deeds and beneficial relationships.

But koinonia also has a more concrete meaning: *Contributions.* In 2 Corinthians, Paul brags that the Macedonians made contributions "beyond their means, begging us earnestly for the privilege of sharing in this ministry" (2 Cor 8:3–4). Their sharing was koinonia, the giving of generous gifts. Such a call to generosity is repeated in Hebrews, which says, "Do not neglect to do good and to share what you have, for such sacrifices are pleasing to God" (Heb 13:16).

Koinonia also means *fellowship.* The Book of Acts says that the first converts to Christianity "devoted themselves to the apostles' teaching and fellowship, to the breaking of bread and the prayers" (Acts 2:42). "God is faithful," says Paul in 1 Corinthians. "By him you were called into the fellowship of his Son" (1 Cor 1:9). And John expresses a desire "that you also may have fellowship with us; and truly our fellowship is with the Father and with his Son Jesus Christ" (1 John 1:3). Koinonia is fellowship—companionship, friendship, comradeship.

Finally, koinonia means *spiritual communion.* "The cup of blessing that we bless, is it not a sharing in the blood of Christ?" Paul asks the Corinthians. "The bread that we break, is it not a sharing in the body of Christ?" (1 Cor 10:16). Paul sees the cup as a koinonia in the blood of Christ and the bread as a koinonia in the body of Christ. When we receive the sacrament called Communion, we are sharing a meal that connects us to Christ and to each other. But the presence of Jesus is not limited to Communion. At the end of 2 Corinthians, Paul offers a set of words that are often used as

Philemon 1-21

a blessing at the end of Christian worship, "The grace of the Lord Jesus Christ, the love of God, and the communion of the Holy Spirit be with all of you" (2 Cor 13:13). Paul's hope is that the communion-fellowship-koinonia of the Spirit will remain with everyone long after they have read his letter. The word koinonia in Philemon is one of the Bible's greatest hits because it challenges us to be committed to generous giving, fellowship, and spiritual communion. When we do this, we are connected to God and to each other, sharing the Christian faith through good deeds and beneficial relationships.

Questions:

1. How does the Christian faith help you to see other people in a new light?
2. Which meaning of the world koinonia is most important to you, and why?
3. What does the communion-fellowship-koinonia of the Spirit mean to you?

58

Hebrews 9:23–28

THE LETTER TO THE Hebrews is the first of the General Epistles, a set of letters that were addressed to a general audience, unlike the letters of the apostle Paul. Hebrews was written to Christians who had grown up Jewish, featuring elements that were connected to the ancient sacrificial system of Israel. According to Hebrews, Jesus Christ "had to become like his brothers and sisters in every respect, so that he might be a merciful and faithful high priest in the service of God, to make a sacrifice of atonement for the sins of the people" (Heb 2:17). He entered "once for all into the Holy Place, not with the blood of goats and calves, but with his own blood, thus obtaining eternal redemption" (Heb 9:12). Jesus "suffered outside the city gate in order to sanctify the people by his own blood" (Heb 13:12). Sacrifice, blood, suffering, death. A sad story—one that we would call a tragedy. So why does it leave us feeling good instead of bad? Why does it make us feel grateful?

Researchers have found that watching a tragedy can actually make us thankful. Journalist Tom Jacobs reports that three of the top ten movies in history—*Gone With the Wind, Doctor Zhivago,* and *Titanic*—fall into the tragedy category. Such stories are sad and end with loss or death. But audiences since the time of the ancient Greeks have loved them. Why is this? Jacobs reports that a team of researchers at Ohio State University have marshaled evidence "that watching tragedy inspires self-reflection, which allows us to re-focus on the people in our lives we might otherwise take for granted." They conclude that the melancholy we feel when watching these stories ultimately provokes "pleasant feelings of gratitude." Tragedies can wake us up, remind us of the fragility of life, and inspire us to count our blessings "with regard to close relationships." At the end of the story, we are grateful for what we have. That's the value of tragedy.[1]

Richard Mouw, the president of Fuller Theological Seminary, says that "on the cross of Calvary, Jesus did something for us that we could never do for ourselves as sinners. He engaged in a transaction that has eternal consequences for our standing before a righteous God." We are drawn to the story of Jesus on the cross because we sense that he did something extraordinary there—something that we, as sinners, could never do for ourselves. Mouw says that he "engaged in a transaction that has eternal consequences," one that changed our relationship with God forever.[2]

The Letter to the Hebrews is built on the foundation of an ancient sacrificial system. Moses took the blood of calves and goats and sprinkled all the people, saying "This is the blood of the covenant that God has ordained for you." In this sacrificial system, "almost everything [was] purified with blood, and without the shedding of blood there [was] no forgiveness of sins" (Heb 9:19–22). We don't live in that ancient world any more, sprinkling blood on people to purify them. But we certainly understand that when a person harms us, we want them to pay—maybe even with blood. When we commit a terrible sin ourselves, we want to offer whatever we can to make things right.

According to Hebrews, Jesus steps right into the middle of this bloody story and offers a new approach. His death on the cross is a single "sacrifice of himself" to remove sin, one that is "offered once to bear the sins of many" (Heb 9:26, 28). He does not "offer himself again and again," as Moses or an ancient high priest would do, "year after year with blood that is not his own" (Heb 9:25). Instead, he now appears "in the presence of God on our behalf" and saves those "who are eagerly waiting for him" (Heb 9:24, 28).

The good news of this tragedy is that Jesus removes sin with a single sacrifice, meaning that we do not have to force others to pay or sacrifice our own blood to make things right. It bears the sins of all of us, and does not have to be offered again and again and again. Best of all, Jesus continues to stand in the presence of God on our behalf, like an advocate or attorney ready to argue our case. He saves all of us who turn to him in faith, eagerly waiting for his help. We need this assistance, because we do not have the ability to fix all of the problems we have created.

1. Jacobs, "Sadness Breeds Gratitude: The Value of Tragedy," § 1.
2. Mouw, "Getting to the Crux of Calvary," § 1.

When burdened by sin and guilt, we can be thankful for Jesus. He is our *advocate*, ready to "appear in the presence of God on our behalf" (Heb 9:24). He is our *substitute*, ready to remove our sin "by the sacrifice of himself" (Heb 9:26). He is our *savior*, ready to rescue "those who are eagerly waiting for him" (Heb 9:28). Advocate, substitute, savior—these are the three sides of Jesus in the tragedy of the cross. This passage from Hebrews is one of the Bible's greatest hits because it tells us the story of how Jesus removed our sins by his sacrifice. We learn that he is ready to argue our case, put himself in our place, and save us from any sin that rips the fabric of our relationships with God and neighbor. As people moved by this story, we are invited to follow him in gratitude and faith.

Questions:

1. What feelings does a tragedy evoke in you?
2. When do you feel the desire for a sacrifice, from yourself or someone else?
3. Which role of Jesus makes you most thankful: Advocate, substitute, or savior?

59

James 5:13–20

LIKE HEBREWS, THE LETTER of James was written to Jewish Christians, and his focus was the proper relationship between faith and action. "Be doers of the word, and not merely hearers," he said to a group of Christians outside of Palestine (Jas 1:22). "Faith by itself, if it has no works, is dead" (Jas 2:17). At the end of the letter, he turned his attention to prayer and asked, "Are any among you sick? They should call for the elders of the church and have them pray over them . . . The prayer of faith will save the sick, and the Lord will raise them up; and anyone who has committed sins will be forgiven" (Jas 5:14–15).

James called for prayer when people were suffering, cheerful, and sick, promising that "the prayer of the righteous is powerful and effective" (Jas 5:16). He was convinced that prayer could have a significant effect on our brain, body, heart, and soul—in bad times and good. And today, medical researchers are catching up with him. Dr. Andrew Newberg of Thomas Jefferson Hospital in Philadelphia has been studying the effect of prayer on the brain for over twenty years. He injects radioactive dye into people and then watches for changes in their heads when they pray. He does not claim that prayer is a cure-all, but he believes that it can be every bit as important as science in helping patients to heal. By praying, he said to *NBC News*, "you can cause a lot of different changes all the way throughout the body, which could have a healing effect."[1]

So how does prayer actually work? What makes it powerful and effective? The power of prayer is not that it changes disease, but that it changes

1. Whitman, "Power of Prayer: What Happens to Your Brain When You Pray?" § 1.

us—the people who pray. When Newberg studied a group of Franciscan nuns who joined together in meditative prayer, he discovered that the area of the brain associated with the sense of self began to "shut down." He saw that in this type of prayer, "You become connected to God. You become connected to the world." Prayer deepens our connection to God and to the world around us, which is related to the insight of James, "The prayer of faith will save the sick, and the Lord will raise them up" (Jas 5:15). Prayer connects us to the sick people in the world around us and raises them into the presence of God.

Prayer changes the people who pray, making them more peaceful and accepting and aligned with their Christian convictions. One of the most well-known modern prayers is the Serenity Prayer, said first by Protestant theologian Reinhold Niebuhr during World War II and now central to the recovery from addiction being achieved in thousands of twelve-step groups: "God, grant me the serenity to accept the things I cannot change, courage to change the things I can, and wisdom to know the difference." Notice that God is not being asked in this prayer to heal anyone miraculously, but is being asked to give people serenity, courage, and wisdom so that they can become well and live life more fully. And since part of the healing process is going to include forgiveness, there needs to be an opportunity for honest confession and pardon. This is why James says, "confess your sins to one another, and pray for one another, so that you may be healed" (Jas 5:16). The Serenity Prayer is said in twelve-step groups across our country and throughout the world, and the result has been sobriety for millions of people.

People who pray for serenity, courage, and wisdom will be given the help they need. Eileen Flanagan, who has written a book on the Serenity Prayer called *The Wisdom to Know the Difference*, quotes a study which found that wise people "are able to step outside themselves and assess a troubling situation with calm reflection. They recast a crisis as a problem to be addressed . . . They take action in situations they can control and accept the inability to do so when matters are outside their control."[2] Prayer helps us to step outside ourselves, assess troubling situations, and take action when we can. But it also helps us to accept the inability to act when situations are outside our control.

In the face of various challenges, prayer helps us to make a positive difference in the world. In his second chapter, James wrote, "If a brother

---

2. Brinton, "Hail Mary never works," § 1.

or sister is naked and lacks daily food, and one of you says to them, 'Go in peace; keep warm and eat your fill,' and yet you do not supply their bodily needs, what is the good of that?" (Jas 2:15–16). Faith without works, he said, "is dead" (Jas 2:17). That is why faithful Christians do more than simply offer hurting people their thoughts and prayers—they summon the courage to provide decent clothing, food, and shelter to the poor of their community. This passage from James is one of the Bible's greatest hits because it tells us that prayer is powerful and effective—capable of connecting us with God and with the world around us. "The prayer of faith will save the sick" (Jas 5:15) by raising them into the presence of God, where forgiveness and healing can be obtained, and also by turning us into people who can make a positive difference in the lives of people around us.

Questions:

1. In your experience, what is the power of prayer?
2. How has prayer changed you as a person, if at all?
3. Where do you see a connection between prayer and action?

60

1 Peter 2:19–25

The apostle Peter wrote his first letter to Christians in Asia Minor, which is now Turkey, in a time of persecution by residents of the Roman Empire. "Conduct yourselves honorably among the Gentiles," he encouraged them, "so that, though they malign you as evildoers, they may see your honorable deeds and glorify God when he comes to judge" (1 Pet 2:12). Then Peter lifted up the example of Christ's suffering, saying that "if you endure when you do right and suffer for it, you have God's approval. For to this you have been called, because Christ also suffered for you, leaving you an example, so that you should follow in his steps" (1 Pet 2:20–21). In this verse, Peter is not saying that suffering is a good thing, a right thing, or a desirable thing. But in every life there is suffering, and God can use even bad times for good. Peter tells us that Jesus "bore our sins in his body on the cross, so that, free from sins, we might live for righteousness; by his wounds you have been healed" (1 Pet 2:24). Jesus took our sins on himself and paid our penalty for all time. The good of our forgiveness came out of the bad of Christ's death on the cross.

Good can come out of our own suffering as well. In 1864, the first Union prisoners arrived at the prisoner-of-war camp at Andersonville, Georgia. This Confederate POW camp has always been notorious, since almost thirteen thousand Union men died there from starvation and illness. But a new side of the story is now being highlighted—one that shows the good that existed in that hell-hole of a camp. According to *The Washington Post*, the first prisoners had to create their own housing by making tents out of blankets or digging into a hillside. The water was polluted, and the food rations were very meager. Some men went crazy as they dreamed about good food and life at home. But others kept hope alive by keeping themselves busy. Some sold each other firewood while others made money by selling eggs, soap, cabbage, and sassafras beer. A private from Massachusetts named W.F. Lyon reported in his journal that, "We had a great many breweries in the prison—in fact, there were a whole lot of breweries and saloon combined, for each one sold his own product."

All this activity gave the prisoners something to do and a sense of a normal life, according to *The Washington Post*, keeping "them alive while they waited to be rescued or paroled." Eric Leonard, the chief of education at the Andersonville National Historic Site, is impressed by what the long-term prisoners decided to do with their food. "By early summer, in the midst of all those dying men and the chaos of prison life, they are planting corn," he said. "They took kernels out of their ration of cornmeal and put them in the ground. That speaks to their knowing they will be there long enough to harvest it. What is corn? It symbolizes hope. It is a remarkable act of hope."[1]

In the middle of the suffering we face, Jesus Christ is like a fellow prisoner of war, giving us a model for keeping hope alive in a time of anguish and despair. "For to this you have been called, because Christ also suffered for you, leaving you an example, so that you should follow in his steps," said Peter (1 Pet 2:21). "When he was abused, he did not return abuse; when he suffered, he did not threaten; but he entrusted himself to the one who judges justly" (1 Peter 2:23). The message here is not that we should invite abuse upon ourselves, but rather that we should never return evil for evil. Our call is to follow Christ's example and become Christians who avoid violence at all costs.

Such an approach is not part of any earthly political agenda, but it is at the heart of God's heavenly kingdom order. According to Stanley Hauerwas and William Willimon of Duke Divinity School, discipleship is extended training in letting go of the ways of the world, and "in relying on God's definition of the direction and meaning of the world—that is, the kingdom of God."[2] As disciples, we are to pray that we can let go of our violent traits and discover nonviolent traits, even when we "endure pain while suffering unjustly" (1 Pet 2:19). Then we practice nonviolence *wherever we can*: at home, at work, in the community, at church. We practice it in *whatever way*

---

1. Wheeler, "Hope amid despair," H8.
2. Hauerwas and Willimon, *Resident Aliens*, 88–89.

we can: with children, spouses, co-workers, and the person sitting next to us in the pew.

"Repeated practice is one of the most basic principles of most spiritual and meditative paths," writes Richard Carlson, Ph.D. "In other words, whatever you practice most is what you will become."[3] As in all things, we become a nonviolent person most successfully by practicing it wherever we can, in whatever way we can, as often as we can. This passage from 1 Peter is one of the Bible's greatest hits because it reminds us that Jesus suffered to free us from sin and left us an example of the good that can come from a life of not returning abuse for abuse. In a remarkable act of hope, he planted the seed of nonviolence within us so that we "might live for righteousness" (1 Pet 2:24).

Questions:

1. When have you done right and suffered for it?
2. In the life of Jesus and in your life, how does good come out of suffering?
3. Where have you seen the power of nonviolence at work?

---

3. Carlson, "Remember that You Become What You Practice Most," 171.

61

2 Peter 3:8–15

THE FIRST LETTER OF Peter encouraged the Christians in Asia Minor to stay the course in the face of persecution as well as milder forms of social boycotting and verbal abuse. "Beloved," says Peter, "do not be surprised at the fiery ordeal that is taking place among you to test you" (1 Pet 4:12). He saw it as an opportunity to share in Christ's suffering, preparing for the day when they could "be glad and shout for joy when his glory is revealed" (1 Pet 4:13). His second letter was written to members of the church who were being led astray by false teachers who denied that the world would be brought to its conclusion by divine judgment. "Understand this," he asserted firmly, "that in the last days scoffers will come, scoffing and indulging their own lusts and saying, 'Where is the promise of his coming? For ever since our ancestors died, all things continue as they were from the beginning of creation!'" (2 Pet 3:3–4). Pointing out that the world and its flow of events seemed to be moving along quite nicely, without cataclysmic fire or dissolution, these teachers sowed seeds of doubt about the coming judgment of God.

But Peter took a strong stand against these scoffers, reminding his fellow Christians "that with the Lord one day is like a thousand years, and a thousand years are like one day" (2 Pet 3:8). He wanted them to see that God's timeframe was not the same as a human timeframe, and that God had an agenda at work: "the Lord is not slow about his promise, as some think of slowness," he argued, "but is patient with you, not wanting any to perish, but all to come to repentance" (2 Pet 3:9). From this perspective, a person could actually "regard the patience of our Lord as salvation" (2

Pet 3:15). Christians ought to continue in their faith and good works, said Peter, leading "lives of holiness and godliness, waiting for and hastening the coming of the day of God" (2 Pet 3:11–12). While they "are waiting for these things," they should strive to be found by the Lord "at peace, without spot or blemish" (2 Pet 3:14). Peter did not want Christians to abandon their faith and righteous living as they waited for the day when "the heavens will be set ablaze and dissolved, and the elements will melt with fire" (2 Pet 3:12).

In the 1990s, Reynolds Price, a professor at Duke University and author of a number of fine novels, received a letter from a medical student named Jim. The student had been diagnosed with cancer, and he wrote to Price for solace since the novelist had published a faith-inspiring account of his own recovery from spinal cancer. The young man had a simple query: "Dear Dr. Price: I want to believe in a God who cares . . . because I may meet him sooner than I had expected. I think I am at the point where I can accept the existence of a God (otherwise I can't explain the origin of the universe . . . but I can't yet believe he cares about us)."

After their initial contact, Price did not hear from him again, but learned several months later that the young man had died. Price then wrote a short book called *Letter to a Man in the Fire*, in which he honestly and compassionately responded to the student's request for spiritual insight. "Dear Jim: It hardly seems appropriate to thank you for letting me know the hard facts of the cancer which has interrupted your medical training . . . I feel some thanks that the even harder questions you ask have pressed on me a need to think my way again, if only in the most personal manner, into the bottomless mystery of suffering . . . What I hear you asking is this: Was our universe created by an intelligent power, and if so, is the Creator conscious of its creatures and benignly concerned for their lives?" Price went on to affirm his strong belief in the existence of God: "What I assert with no serious doubt is that our one universe was created and is maintained by a single divine intelligence who still exists and continues to oversee his primeval handiwork."[1]

Like Reynolds Price, the apostle Peter was writing a letter to people in the fire. And what both writers tell us is that God is powerful, but unpredictable, and that God is concerned for our lives, but not likely to protect us from every form of stress. God is sometimes quick to act and sometimes patient and long-suffering; mysterious, but also revealed as the Creator; capable of judging harshly and decisively, but also lavish in his great and

---

1. Price, *Letter to a Man in the Fire*, 23–27.

unexpected mercy. Whatever fire we face, God desires the best for us. "It's not the nature of love to create and then annihilate," said the novelist Madeleine L'Engle. "If I believe God is love, then I have to believe that what has been made is going to go on being made."[2] The Christian mystic Julian of Norwich reminded us that our Lord never said: You will not be troubled, you will not be belabored, you will not be afflicted. But he said: You will not be overcome.[3] This passage from 2 Peter is one of the Bible's greatest hits because it promises us that God is with us in the face of any fire, and we can "regard the patience of the Lord as salvation" (2 Pet 3:15). Although God's timeframe is not the same as ours, we can trust that God's loving agenda is always at work.

Questions:

1. When have you faced a trial by fire, and what was the outcome?
2. What problems arise when we try to align God's timeframe with our own?
3. How is God's nature revealed to you in times of personal difficulty?

---

2. L'Engle, "What Happens After Death?" 95–96.
3. Julian of Norwich in *Handbook for Mortals*, 33.

62

1 John 4:7–21

"You shall love your neighbor as yourself" (Lev 19:18). That's what God said to the people of Israel in the Bible's greatest hit from the book of Leviticus. As far as formulas go, it's terrific. For thousands of years, it has worked well in most of the world's religions. Hindus affirm that "one should not behave toward others in a way which is disagreeable to oneself." Buddhists say that you should "hurt not others in ways that you yourself would find hurtful." And Muslims believe that "no one of you is a believer until he desires for his brother that which he desires for himself." Even Jesus endorsed it when he made it a part of his great commandment, the Bible's greatest hit from Matthew. "Love the Lord your God," said Jesus, and "love your neighbor as yourself" (Matt 22:37, 39).

But surprisingly, in the first of his New Testament letters, the apostle John offers a new recipe: "Beloved, let us love one another, because love is from God; everyone who loves is born of God and knows God. Whoever does not love does not know God, for God is love" (1 John 4:7–8). In these verses, John challenges us to love one another, just as the great religions of the world recommend. But this new approach includes the statement "love is from God" along with the bold assertion that "God is love." That's a whole new formula, combining the commandment to love with the identity of God.

In recent years, companies have learned how dangerous it is to change the ingredients of a successful brand. In April 1985, Coca-Cola changed its formula and introduced a product called "New Coke." The response was overwhelmingly negative, and within three months the original formula was back on the market. Surprisingly, Coke decided to change its formula again in 2013, offering a new version called "Coca-Cola Life." It gets its sweetness from sugar and stevia, which is derived from a plant in the chrysanthemum family, reducing the calorie count per can.[1] "Life" has received mixed reviews around the world, highlighting the danger of changing a successful brand.

So why does John change the love formula? For starters, he wants to put a human face on the commandment to love one another—the face of Jesus Christ. "God's love was revealed among us in this way: God sent his only Son into the world so that we might live through him. In this is love, not that we loved God but that he loved us and sent his Son to be the atoning sacrifice for our sins" (1 John 4:9–10). John knows that the problem with the love commandment is that it can easily become too sweet, with people enjoying the pleasant taste of tender emotions and charitable thoughts. So he changes the formula to include the atoning sacrifice of Christ on the cross.

Such a change of ingredients can have a powerful impact. "Beloved, since God loved us so much, we also ought to love one another. No one has ever seen God; if we love one another, God lives in us, and his love is perfected in us" (1 John 4:11–12). Under this new formula, the loving sacrifice of Christ becomes the model for our loving sacrifices for one another. "We love because he first loved us," says John. Those "who love God must love their brothers and sisters also" (1 John 4:19–21). When we show this kind of love, God actually lives in us, and God's love is perfected in us.

In my novel *City of Peace*, a pastor named Harley Camden makes a visit to jail to see an inmate named Muhammad Bayati, accused of murdering his daughter. The two begin to talk about their beliefs, and Muhammad says, "God is merciful and just."

"God is also love," adds Harley. "Our Bible says that God is love."

Muhammad cocks his head slightly. "That is different from our understanding. We have many names for God, but love is not among them."

"For Christians, love is at the core of who God is," explains Harley. "God reveals his love by sending Jesus to bring us forgiveness and new life. And the response we are supposed to make is to love one another—a love that should be extended to friends, enemies, blacks, whites, Muslims, Jews, fellow Christians. It is all supposed to come down to love. In fact, the Bible insists that those who say, 'I love God' but hate their brothers and sisters, are liars."

---

1. Hofherr, "Is the new Coca-Cola 'Life' healthier than regular Coke?" § 1.

"I would agree with that," says Muhammad. "Loving God does require that we love the people around us."[2]

This passage from 1 John is one of the Bible's greatest hits because it reveals for the first time that "God is love" and promises that "those who abide in love abide in God, and God abides in them" (1 John 4:16). To abide is to live or to dwell in something—to accept, observe, and follow a particular path. For John, to love God is to love our brothers and sisters, and to abide in love is to abide in God, with no distinction between the two. This is a brand-new formula for life with God, one that is based on the love God has for each and every one of us.

Questions:

1. What is the significance of John's insight that God is love?
2. How is the sacrifice of Jesus on the cross a sign of God's love for us?
3. What does it mean to you to abide in love and abide in God?

---

2. Brinton, *City of Peace*, 77.

63

2 John 4–11

THE SECOND LETTER OF John was written to "the elect lady and her children, whom I love in the truth" (2 John 1). This "lady" was probably a local congregation, not an individual, and "her children" were members of the church. He began by saying that he was "overjoyed to find some of your children walking in the truth" (2 John 4), followed by the words "and now, dear lady, I am not writing you a new command but one that we have had from the beginning. I ask that we love one another" (2 John 5). John had a focus on love and truth in this very short letter, only thirteen verses in length. In fact, it is the shortest book in the Bible, although the fifteen verses of John's third letter actually contain fewer words.

John challenged this community to "love one another," as he had commanded Christians to do in his first letter. Then he defined love by saying, "And this is love, that we walk according to [God's] commandments; this is the commandment just as you have heard it from the beginning—you must walk in it" (2 John 6). Love is much more than an emotion in John's understanding, and it includes walking according to God's commands and walking in the truth of what God has revealed in Jesus. This is an active and sacrificial love, one that Jesus described in the Gospel of John when he said, "This is my commandment, that you love one another as I have loved you. No one has greater love than this, to lay down one's life for one's friends" (John 15:12–13).

But who are the friends of Jesus? John wrote this letter because a group had left the Christian community, and he felt that they were no longer adhering to the truth of Christ. "Many deceivers have gone out into the world, those who do not confess that Jesus Christ has come in the flesh," said John; "any such person is the deceiver and the antichrist! Be on your guard, so that you do not lose what we have worked for, but may receive a full reward" (2 John 7–8). John wanted the faithful friends of Jesus to be on guard against people who denied that Jesus had been fully human, perhaps preaching that he only seemed to be human. This splinter group may have been "progressive innovators," according to New Testament scholar Raymond Brown, causing John to issue the warning, "Everyone who does not abide in the teaching of Christ, but goes beyond it, does not have God" (2 John 9). These innovators went beyond the teaching of Christ by "neglecting the 'flesh' or humanity of Jesus."[1]

Affirming that Jesus Christ "has come in the flesh" is an ongoing challenge in the life of the church. For years, the Christian faith has focused on the soul and has seen the flesh as something less important—sometimes even totally depraved. Even though the Nicene Creed says that Jesus "was made man," many Christians have a negative view of human flesh. Neither Jesus nor the Jews wanted this split between body and spirit to exist, but a group of Greek thinkers in the early church introduced a dualistic philosophy that had a negative view of the body and a positive view of the spirit. Later theologians developed this theme: Saint Augustine believed that the soul makes war with the body, and the Protestant reformer John Calvin saw earthly human existence as "a rottenness and a worm."

Jesus, like his Jewish colleagues, saw the flesh as a good gift of God, and he rejoiced in the pleasures of touch and taste and other bodily sensations. "From the beginning Christianity has been an incarnational faith—'the Word became flesh,'" says Monsignor Bill Parent, "which means that there is something fundamentally good about our human flesh." Fortunately, more and more people today are eager to make a connection between body and spirit, and many are pursuing this goal through diet and exercise. Suddenly we have churches offering "Christian Yoga," which presents elements of the Hindu practice of hatha yoga in a Christ-centered setting. Others feature weight-loss classes with names like "Jesus Is the Weigh" and "Weigh Down Workshop" (which has been offered in at least ten thousand churches), and book publishers are turning out titles such as *The Maker's Diet*, outlining a "Biblically correct" eating plan. After two thousand years of being largely separated, spirit and body are finally coming back together.[2]

1. Brown, *The Churches the Apostles Left Behind*, 110–11.
2. Brinton, "What Would Jesus Weigh?" § 1.

2 John 4-11

The reunion of spirit and body carries with it the possibility of integrity—that is, the bringing together of different parts into a unified whole. As human beings, we long to be complete and undivided, enjoying integrity as physical, emotional, intellectual, sexual, and spiritual creatures. John was advocating integrity when he pointed to the teaching of Christ and said, "whoever abides in the teaching has both the Father and the Son. Do not receive into the house or welcome anyone who comes to you and does not bring this teaching" (2 John 9-10). This passage from 2 John is one of the Bible's greatest hits because it is grounded in the belief that Jesus was fully human and fully God, and it challenges us to exercise our bodies and spirits by "walking in the truth" (2 John 4).

Questions:

1. Where do you see a connection between love and truth?
2. What significance do you attach to the humanity of Jesus?
3. How do you make an effort to keep body and spirit together?

64

3 John 1–8

THE THIRD LETTER OF John was written to an individual described as "the beloved Gaius, whom I love in the truth" (3 John 1). John wrote this personal letter to warn him about the danger of an insubordinate leader "who likes to put himself first" and had been "spreading false charges against us" (3 John 9–10)—a reminder to us that there has been conflict in the church since its earliest days. But before issuing this warning, John commended Gaius by saying, "I was overjoyed when some of the friends arrived and testified to your faithfulness to the truth, namely how you walk in the truth. I have no greater joy than this, to hear that my children are walking in the truth" (3 John 3–4). Once again, John focused his attention on the truth of the Christian faith and commended Gaius and his fellow church members for "walking in the truth."

Quinn McDowell is an assistant men's basketball coach at Lehigh University, a man who played basketball at William and Mary before graduating in 2012 with a degree in religious studies. He writes that effective leaders "are constantly trying to match their words with their actions. Ultimately, this process builds trust and earns credibility. Trust is earned when the leader is able to *both* walk the walk and talk the talk... Learning to *walk the walk* and *talk the talk* is about the crucial work of creating alignment between what we say and what we do."[1] This kind of alignment was exactly what John was recommending when he spoke of "walking in the truth" (3 John 4)—an alignment of feet, head, and heart that is critical for leaders of churches as well as basketball teams.

---

1. McDowell, "Walk the Walk, Talk the Talk," § 1.

3 John 1-8

So, what impressed John about the leadership of Gaius? In particular, his practice of Christian hospitality. "Beloved, you do faithfully whatever you do for the friends, even though they are strangers to you," wrote John; "they have testified to your love before the church. You will do well to send them on in a manner worthy of God; for they began their journey for the sake of Christ, accepting no support from non-believers" (3 John 5-7). Gaius had welcomed a group of John's friends, even though they were strangers to him, and John reported that they had testified to Gaius's love. The Greek word for hospitality is *philoxenia,* which means "love of the stranger," shown when Gaius welcomed strangers (*xenous*) and showed them love. How different this is from the *xenophobia* seen in so many communities today, a Greek word which means "fear of the stranger."

One of the central truths of the ministry of Jesus was hospitality, a truth that he both walked and talked. In the Gospel of John, Jesus performed his first miracle at a wedding in Cana, turning more than one hundred gallons of water into wine so that a wedding celebration could continue (John 2:1-11). At its most basic level, this was a miracle of hospitality. Jesus went on to feed crowds of five thousand and then four thousand, revealing his desire to nourish people both physically and spiritually. He washed the feet of his disciples, instituted the Lord's Supper, and after his resurrection, cooked a fish breakfast for his disciples (John 21:1-14). Jesus taught us what it means to care for each other in the parable of the Good Samaritan, welcomed little children in spite of his disciples' objections, and instructed his followers in the nature of hospitality with the words, "when you give a banquet, invite the poor, the crippled, the lame, and the blind" (Luke 14:13).

In a word, a central truth of Jesus was "hospitality." But his walking in this truth was not a punch-and-cookies hospitality; it was a powerful hospitality that stood up to opposition. When the Pharisees asked why Jesus ate with tax collectors and sinners, he said, "Those who are well have no need of a physician, but those who sick" (Matt 9:11-12). He called out to a notorious tax collector named Zacchaeus and invited himself to dinner (Luke 19:1-10). Throughout his ministry, Jesus entered into the lives of people who were on the margins of society, struggling with hunger, shame, and disease. Then, in the Gospel of Matthew, Jesus said that anyone who feeds the hungry and welcomes strangers is really feeding and welcoming him (Matt 25:39).[2]

---

2. Brinton, "Christian Truth, Muscular Hospitality, and the Reception of Refugees," § 1.

If Christians today are going to model their ministries on the work of Jesus, they need to enter into the lives of distressed neighbors and practice hospitality in the same way that Jesus did. "Therefore we ought to support such people," concluded John, "so that we may become co-workers with the truth" (3 John 8). To be co-workers with the truth of Jesus means to practice Christian hospitality and welcome all people with God's love and grace. This passage from 3 John is one of the Bible's greatest hits because it challenges us to reach out actively to the strangers around us. The truth of Christianity is not just talk, but is "walking the walk" with a welcoming way of life, following the Christ who is "the way, the truth, and the life" (John 14:6).

Questions:

1. What are the challenges of walking the walk and talking the talk?
2. Where do you see a need for the powerful hospitality of Jesus today?
3. How can you be a coworker with the truth of Christian hospitality?

65

Jude 3–13

THE AUTHOR OF THIS short letter was Jude, "a servant of Jesus Christ," and he was writing to "those who are called, who are beloved in God the Father and kept safe for Jesus Christ" (Jude 1). Like John, he was addressing a church in conflict, and he spoke with concern about intruders "who pervert the grace of our God into licentiousness and deny our only Master and Lord, Jesus Christ" (Jude 4). He warned his fellow Christians about false teachers who made the case that God's grace could be used as an excuse to practice "licentiousness," immoral living, which he saw as a denial of the lordship of Christ. Jude grounded his thoughts in Scripture, which for him and members of the early church was the whole Hebrew Bible. In similar manner, Christians today are challenged to be attentive to the Bible in its entirety, which is why my book contains what I consider to be the top sixty-six passages from *all of Scripture*, Genesis to Revelation.

"Now I desire to remind you," wrote Jude, "though you are fully informed, that the Lord, who once for all saved a people out of the land of Egypt, afterward destroyed those who did not believe" (Jude 5). He was reminding them of the Bible's greatest hit from the Book of Exodus, which showed the power of God to overcome oppression and lead people to new life. Jude also said that the Lord "afterward destroyed those who did not believe," reminding his readers of the disbelief and disobedience of the Israelites wandering in the wilderness. He may have been referring to stories from the Book of Numbers, including the greatest hit of Numbers chapter 21, in which the people spoke against God and Moses, causing God to send poisonous serpents among the people, leading to many deaths. New

Testament scholar Duane Watson points out that Jude was teaching that Christians, "like the wilderness generation, can lose their salvation and become the object of judgment for their unbelief and disobedience."[1]

Jude then told the story of "the angels who did not keep their own position, but left their proper dwelling" (Jude 6). These angels were mentioned in the Book of Genesis as "the sons of God who went in to the daughters of humans" (Gen 6:4), creatures who left their proper place in heaven to have sex with humans on earth. Jude condemned this sexual activity and said that God had kept them "in eternal chains in deepest darkness for the judgment of the great Day" (Jude 6). In his mind, this story was a strong warning about intruders in the church "who long ago were designated for this condemnation as ungodly, who pervert the grace of our God into licentiousness" (Jude 4). Continuing this theme, Jude reminded his fellow Christians of how "Sodom and Gomorrah and the surrounding cities, which, in the same manner as they, indulged in sexual immorality and pursued unnatural lust, serve as an example by undergoing a punishment of eternal fire" (Jude 7). Again, he went back to the Book of Genesis to find an ancient story that could guide his fellow Christians.

Stories have been a powerful teaching tool through the history of our faith. Remember King David and the Bible's greatest hit from 2 Samuel? After David committed adultery with Bathsheba and arranged for her husband to be killed, God sent the prophet Nathan to David. He said to the king: "There were two men in a certain city, one rich and the other poor. The rich man had very many flocks and herds; but the poor man had nothing but one little ewe lamb, which he had bought . . . Now there came a traveler to the rich man, and he was loath to take one of his own flock or herd to prepare for the wayfarer who had come to him, but he took the poor man's lamb, and prepared that for the guest who had come to him." Then David, feeling rage toward the man, said to Nathan, "As the Lord lives, the man who has done this deserves to die." Nathan said to David, "You are the man!" (2 Sam 12:1–7). The prophet did not condemn David with a quotation from the Ten Commandments, noting the rules against murder and adultery. Instead, he told him a story which acted as a mirror, helping David to see himself clearly.

We are story-telling animals. In his book *After Virtue: A Study in Moral Theology*, philosopher Alasdair MacIntyre wrote that a human being is "a teller of stories that aspire to truth." The Bible is just such a set of

---

1. Watson, "The Letter of Jude," 488.

Jude 3-13

stories, and its narratives reveal to us what is true about our faith, our community, and ourselves.[2] This passage from Jude is one of the Bible's greatest hits because it gives Christians guidance about how they should act, based on stories from Holy Scripture. Because the recipients of Jude's letter knew the Bible well, they understood his warnings about false teachers, "Woe to them! For they go the way of Cain, and abandon themselves to Balaam's error for the sake of gain, and perish in Korah's rebellion" (Jude 11). By rooting ourselves securely in the stories of Scripture, we avoid their fate as "waterless clouds carried along by the winds; autumn trees without fruit, twice dead, uprooted; wild waves of the sea, casting up the foam of their own shame" (Jude 12–13).

Questions:

1. What is the value of looking at the whole Bible instead of individual verses?
2. Where do you find guidance for sexual morality in Scripture?
3. Why are stories, as opposed to commandments, such powerful teaching tools?

---

2. Brinton, "Fiction in faith formation: Stories that act as mirrors," § 2.

66

Revelation 21:1–4; 22:1–7

THE BOOK OF REVELATION is filled with frightening images: A great red dragon, beasts from the sea and land, the bowls of God's wrath, a great whore, an apocalyptic battle, and the final judgment. When the seventh trumpet blows, we learn of God's plan "for destroying those who destroy the earth" (Rev 11:18). American pop-culture has picked up on these horrors, such as in the apocalyptic comedy *This Is the End* (2013), in which Los Angeles is destroyed by earthquakes and the righteous are taken to heaven in beams of blue light. Jokes about the end-times have been around since *Ghostbusters* (1984), in which a character says, "Fire and brimstone coming down from the skies! Rivers and seas boiling! Forty years of darkness! Earthquakes, volcanoes . . . The dead rising from the grave! Human sacrifice, dogs and cats living together . . . mass hysteria!"

That's pop-eschatology, and a lot of it is grounded in the vision of John in Revelation. (Except perhaps for the "dogs and cats living together.") And much ink has been spilled by scholars trying to figure it all out. But destruction, doom, and damnation are not the final word in Revelation. Instead, the book ends with a vision of a new heaven and a new earth, and the restoration of the Garden of Eden. The promise of the last two chapters of Revelation is a new relationship with God, one that is both intimate and eternal, in which people live in harmony with God and with all that God has made. This bond is a restoration of the original creation in Genesis, and it contains the best of numerous biblical images—a new heaven and earth, a city, and a garden.

Revelation 21:1–4; 22:1–7

First, *new heaven and earth*. As chapter 21 begins, John sees "a new heaven and a new earth; for the first heaven and the first earth had passed away, and the sea was no more" (Rev 21:1). This new creation is one in which the past is forgotten, and even the sea, which is a symbol of watery chaos, is "no more." This transformed creation fulfills the expectation of the apostle Paul that "the creation itself will be set free from its bondage to decay" (Rom 8:21). In so many ways, we struggle today with a creation that is in bondage to decay. We look around and see the fouling of air, land, and water. We look at our relationships and see brokenness between friends, colleagues, spouses, and family members. We look inside ourselves and see the decay of our morals and our aspirations. There is hope to be found in this vision of a new heaven and earth, in which the creation itself will be liberated from decay.

Second, *a city*. John sees "the holy city, the New Jerusalem, coming down out of heaven from God, prepared as a bride adorned for her husband" (Rev 21:2). New Jerusalem is the new relationship that God has made with the followers of Christ—Paul says that this Jerusalem from above "is free, and she is our mother" (Gal 4:26). This holy city is the beautiful place where God and humans will live together eternally—a city that descends to earth instead of remaining in heaven. "See, the home of God is among mortals," says a voice from the throne. "God himself will be with them" (Rev 21:3). God chooses to live among people, in a restored and renewed paradise on earth.

Third, Revelation speaks of *a garden*—a Garden of Eden, restored in the center of the city. This is a powerful message about God's desire for the human world to exist in harmony with nature, and it serves as biblical support for the church's commitment to the stewardship of the earth. In this urban garden, we hear an echo of the creation story from Genesis, in which a "river flows out of Eden to water the garden" (Gen 2:10). In Revelation, an angel shows John "the river of the water of life, bright as crystal, flowing from the throne of God and of the Lamb through the middle of the street of the city" (Rev 22:1–2). On the banks of the river is the tree of life, "and the leaves of the tree are for the healing of the nations" (Rev 22:2). Best of all, "the throne of God and of the Lamb will be in it, and his servants will worship him; they will see his face" (Rev 22:3–4). Faithful people will finally encounter God and Christ directly, as the apostle Paul dreamed when he wrote, "For now we see in a mirror, dimly, but then we will see face to face" (1 Cor 13:12). The light of God will shine directly on those who worship

God, and together the Lord and his servants will "reign forever and ever" (Rev 22:5).

Revelation tells us that God has a plan "for destroying those who destroy the earth," but the horror of this outcome can be avoided (Rev 11:18). This passage is one of the Bible's greatest hits because it tells us that we can restore the earth by creating communities that reflect the values of God's garden in the city—places in which healthy relationships exist between people and nature, as well as between people and God.[1] Such harmony is the goal of all of the books of the Bible, expressed in a variety of ways by a wide range of voices, from Genesis to Revelation. "These words are trustworthy and true," says the angel of Revelation, now and always. "Blessed is the one who keeps the words of the prophecy of this book" (Rev 22:6–7).

Questions:

1. Why do you think the frightening images of Revelation are so memorable?
2. What hope do you find in the new heaven and earth, the city, and the garden?
3. How will you keep the words of this book, along with other biblical books?

---

1. Brinton, "Between Text and Sermon: Revelation 21:1—22:7," 84–86.

Epilogue

CONGRATULATIONS ON COMPLETING THIS journey through the Bible, from the first day of creation to a new heaven and a new earth. You have experienced a wide range of essential passages, and have probably picked up on themes that run through the entirety of Scripture: God's word, liberation, law, covenant, commandment, repentance, justice, righteousness, faith, and love. I hope that you have discovered the depth of the relationship between the Old Testament and the New, and the ways in which verses in one biblical book are echoed in another. Yes, the "wind from God [that] swept over the face of the waters" (Gen 1:2) is the very same Spirit that came to earth with the sound of a mighty wind on the Day of Pentecost (Acts 2:1–4), and the prophet Habakkuk's understanding that "the righteous live by their faith" (Hab 2:4) is the inspiration for the apostle Paul's insight that "a person is justified by faith apart from works prescribed by the law" (Rom 3:28). The divine word "let there be light" (Gen 1:3) is the Word who "was in the beginning with God" (John 1:2), and this Word became flesh in Jesus Christ (John 1:14), in whom "all things in heaven and on earth were created" (Col 1:16). From a Christian perspective, Jesus is the one in whom "all things hold together" (Col 1:17).

While the greatest hits of the Bible hold together in a remarkable way, there is also diversity in Scripture. God's truth is spoken in a variety of voices, and sometimes they contradict each other. The exclusiveness of the Book of Ezra, with a denunciation of marriages between Israelites and other tribes, is at odds with the more inclusive message of the Book of Ruth, in which a Moabite woman becomes the great-grandmother of King David. Paul's assertion that Abraham's "faith was reckoned to him as righteousness" (Rom 4:22) stands in creative tension with the statement of James that "faith by itself, if it has no works, is dead" (Jas 2:17). The power of Scripture is that it allows the truth of God to be revealed in different ways, and does not require us to provide simple answers to complex questions. In the life of the church, we know that it is important to maintain particular practices and traditions (exclusiveness) at the very same time that we open our doors to people of different races and cultures (inclusiveness). We can hold to the belief that we are saved by the grace of God through our faith in Christ, while also doing good work as the hands and feet of Jesus in the world today. David's sexual abuse of Bathsheba is a cautionary tale in 2 Samuel, but this story does not mean that God is anti-sex, as the erotic love poem of the Song of Solomon makes abundantly clear. The truth of Scripture is a multi-faceted gem, as I hope you have discovered through these sixty-six greatest hits.

Many of these passages have come as no surprise to you, I am sure, but I hope that some have appeared as hidden gems. The book of the prophet Obadiah and the letter of Jude rarely appear in sermons or Bible studies, but they have a message for anyone who takes the time to read them. One of the joys of researching this book was the challenge of finding greatest hits in the most obscure books of the Bible, such as the shortest letter (2 John) and the book jammed with genealogies (1 Chronicles). But in each one I found a treasure, and it was a pleasure to present it to you. Now, I invite you to go back through the Bible and look for other classic passages, since even the most comprehensive of greatest hits collections is going to omit a few top tunes. I lifted up the creation story from Genesis, but what about God's covenant with Abraham? I highlighted the love chapter from 1 Corinthians, but maybe I should have chosen Paul's important message about the power of the cross. What is the greatest hit of the Gospel of Luke: The birth of Jesus in Bethlehem, the beginning of his ministry, the parable of the Good Samaritan, or the walk to Emmaus? I could pick only one. Whether you have read this book as a private devotional or used it in a Bible study class, I invite you to consider it to be a starting point for continued engagement with Scripture. Go back into the sixty-six books of the Bible, find other passages that are truly great, and let their messages challenge and inspire you. You'll find that the hits continue to appear, as God speaks to you from the entirety of the Bible, Genesis to Revelation.

Bibliography

Alexander, Julia. "The Office's John Krasinski launched a YouTube channel dedicated to good news." *The Verge*, March 30, 2020. https://www.theverge.com/2020/3/30/21200161/john-krasinski-youtube-some-good-news-office-steve-carell-michael-scott-coronavirus.

Are Jr. Tom. "Job 38:1–7." *Interpretation*. July 1999, 295.

Baard, Erik. "Smart bricks, or a dumb idea?" *Wired*, June 20, 2003. https://www.wired.com/2003/06/smart-bricks-or-a-dumb-idea/.

Bainton, Roland. *Here I Stand*. Nashville: Abingdon, [1950], 1978.

Bell, Rob. *Love Wins: A Book About Heaven, Hell, and the Fate of Every Person Who Ever Lived*. New York: HarperOne, 2011.

Birch, Bruce C. "The First and Second Books of Samuel." *The New Interpreter's Bible*. Nashville: Abingdon, 1998.

Bobb, David J. *Humility: An Unlikely Biography of America's Greatest Virtue*. Nashville: Thomas Nelson, 2013.

Boyd, Gregory. "Created for community." *Christian Century*, May 19, 2009, 20–21.

Branch, Taylor. *Parting the Waters: America in the King Years 1954–63*. New York: Simon and Schuster, 1988.

Braverman, Beth. "The 10 most dangerous jobs in America." *CNBC*, December 28, 2919. https://www.cnbc.com/2019/12/27/the-10-most-dangerous-jobs-in-america-according-to-bls-data.html.

Brinton, Henry G. *Balancing Acts: Obligation, Liberation, And Contemporary Christian Conflicts*. Lima, OH: CSS, 2006.

———. "Between Text and Sermon: Revelation 21:1—22:7." *Interpretation*, January 2016, 84–86.

———. "Christian Truth, Muscular Hospitality, and the Reception of Refugees." *Huffington Post*, November 23, 2015. https://www.huffpost.com/entry/christian-truth-muscular-_b_8623686.

———. *City of Peace*. Virginia Beach, VA: Köehler, 2018.

———. "False idols come in many guises." *USA TODAY*, September 1, 2014, 8A.

———. "Fiction in faith formation: Stories that act as mirrors." *The Presbyterian Outlook*, December 30, 2019. https://pres-outlook.org/2019/12/fiction-in-faith-formation-stories-that-act-as-mirrors/.

———. "Hail Mary never works." *USA TODAY*, February 2, 2014. https://www.usatoday.com/story/opinion/2014/02/02/super-bowl-broncos-seahawks-god-american-atheists-column/5162055/.

Bibliography

———. *The Welcoming Congregation: Roots and Fruits of Christian Hospitality.* Louisville: Westminster John Knox, 2012.

———. "What Would Jesus Weigh?" *The Washington Post,* July 18, 2004. https://www.washingtonpost.com/archive/opinions/2004/07/18/what-would-jesus-weigh/c15af732-cd12-4cbf-b19f-a4523ddd73c7/.

Brinton, Henry G. and John Y.H. Yieh. *Revelation: Immersion Bible Studies.* Nashville: Abingdon, 2011.

Brown, Raymond E. *The Churches the Apostles Left Behind.* New York: Paulist, 1984.

Brueggemann, Walter. *An Introduction to the Old Testament.* Louisville: Westminster John Knox, 2003.

Buechner, Frederick, quoted by Rick Christian. *The One Year Alive Devotions for Students.* Carol Stream, IL: Tyndale House, 2014.

Calvin, John. *Commentary on the Book of Psalms.* Grand Rapids, MI: Baker Book House, 1979.

———. *Institutes of the Christian Religion*: Book One, Chapter 1, https://reformed.org/wp-content/uploads/2019/04/Calvin-Institutes-of-Christian-Religion.pdf.

Carlson, Richard. "Remember that You Become What You Practice Most." In *Don't Sweat the Small Stuff . . . and It's All Small Stuff.* New York: Hyperion, 1997.

Childs, Brevard S. *Isaiah.* Louisville: Westminster John Knox, 2001.

Chokshi, Niraj. "Fear of a vengeful God may explain global humanity's expansion." *The Washington Post,* February 12, 2016. https://www.washingtonpost.com/news/acts-of-faith/wp/2016/02/12/fear-of-a-vengeful-god-may-explain-humanitys-global-expansion/.

Claiborne, Shane. *Irresistible Revolution: living as an ordinary radical.* Grand Rapids: Zondervan, 2006.

Dean, Cordelia. "When cancer strikes, a high achiever plans." *The New York Times,* March 14, 2006, D7.

Delaney, Kevin J. "Plato's Greek Is Legible at Last on Modern PCs." *The Wall Street Journal,* February 22, 2000, B1.

Dickson, John. "Great Humility." *Leadership Journal,* Winter 2012. https://www.christianitytoday.com/pastors/2012/winter/greathumility.html.

Eastman, Susan Grove. "Love's Folly: Love and Knowledge in 1 Corinthians." *Interpretation,* January 2018, 14.

Eckelmeyer, Judith. "On Hearing the 'Christmas' Portion of Handel's *Messiah*." *Music Academy Online.* http://musicacademyonline.com/programs/messiah_01.php.

Ehrman, Bart D. "The Myths of Jesus." *Newsweek,* December 17, 2012, 24–28.

Ewert, David. "Vengeance." *The Oxford Companion to the Bible.* New York: Oxford University Press, 1993.

Fears, Darryl. "Invasive bugs making a bigger stink." *The Washington Post,* August 8, 2011, A1.

Frykholm, Amy. "Countering the darkness." *Christian Century,* July 8, 2015, 10.

García-Treto, Francisco O. "The Book of Nahum." *The New Interpreter's Bible.* Nashville: Abingdon, 1996.

Gilbert, Greg. "Book Review: The Prayer of Jabez by Bruce Wilkinson." *9Marks,* March 3, 2010. https://www.9marks.org/review/prayer-jabez-bruce-wilkinson/.

Gladwell, Malcolm. "How David Beats Goliath." *The New Yorker,* May 11, 2009. https://www.newyorker.com/magazine/2009/05/11/how-david-beats-goliath.

Bibliography

Grolle, Johann. "Nobel Physicist Frank Wilczek: 'The world is a piece of art.'" *SPIEGEL Online International,* August 21, 2015. https://www.spiegel.de/international/physicist-frank-wilczek-interview-about-beauty-in-physics-a-1048669.html.

Hauerwas, Stanley and William H. Willimon. *Resident Aliens: Life in the Christian Colony.* Nashville: Abingdon, 1989.

Hays, Richard B. "The Letter to the Galatians." *The New Interpreter's Bible.* Nashville: Abingdon, 2000.

———. "The word of reconciliation." *Faith & Leadership,* July 19, 2010. https://faithandleadership.com/word-reconciliation.

Hofherr, Justine. "Is the new Coca-Cola 'Life' healthier than regular Coke? (And will it come to the US?)." *Boston.com,* June 17, 2014. https://www.boston.com/news/business/2014/06/17/is-the-new-coca-cola-life-healthier-than-regular-coke-and-will-it-come-to-the-us. "New Coke." https://en.wikipedia.org/wiki/New_Coke.

Hollaway, Steve. "Let Justice and Righteousness Flow: Making Things Right and Doing Right." *The Block Island Times,* January 17, 2016. https://www.blockislandtimes.com/affiliate-post/let-justice-and-righteousness-flow-making-things-right-and-doing-right/45390.

Huyser-Honig, Joan. "Eric Washington on God's Sovereignty and Slavery." *Calvin Institute of Christian Worship,* April 24, 2015. https://worship.calvin.edu/resources/resource-library/eric-washington-on-god-s-sovereignty-and-slavery/.

Jacobs, Tom. "Sadness Breeds Gratitude: The Value of Tragedy." *Miller-McCune Website,* March 15, 2012. https://psmag.com/social-justice/sadness-breeds-gratitude-the-value-of-tragedy-40387.

Jenkins, Philip. *The New Faces of Christianity: Believing the Bible in the Global South.* Oxford: Oxford University Press, 2006.

Julian of Norwich, quoted by Joanne Lynn and Joan Harrold. *Handbook for Mortals.* New York: Oxford University Press, 1999.

King Jr., Martin Luther. "I've Been to the Mountaintop." *The Martin Luther King, Jr. Research and Education Institute,* April 3, 1968. https://kinginstitute.stanford.edu/encyclopedia/ive-been-mountaintop.

———. "What Dr. King Wrote, and What He Did." *The New York Times,* November 13, 1990, 30.

Kingsley, Regeena. "What are 'Rules of Engagement'? Military Mandates & Instructions for the Use of Force." *Military Caveats,* http://militarycaveats.com/9-what-are-rules-of-engagement/.

Klein, Ralph W. "The Books of Ezra and Nehemiah." *New Interpreter's Bible.* Nashville: Abingdon, 1999.

Latson, Jennifer. "How FDR's Radio Voice Solved a Banking Crisis." *Time,* March 12, 2015. https://time.com/3731744/fdr-fireside-chat-banking/.

L'Engle, Madeline. "What Happens After Death?" *Questions of Faith.* Philadelphia: Trinity Press International, 1990.

Lewis, C.S. *Mere Christianity.* New York: HarperCollins, 1952.

Lewis, Dean H. "The Presbyterian-Reformed Church in Cuba (IPRC)." *Cuba Partners Network,* https://cubapartnersnetwork.org/history/iprc-history/.

Lomas, Tim. "The Magic of 'Untranslatable' Words." *Scientific American,* July 12, 2016. https://www.scientificamerican.com/article/the-magic-of-untranslatable-words/.

Long, Thomas G. "Preaching Romans Today." *Interpretation,* July 2004, 273.

Bibliography

Lose, David J. "Homiletical Perspective: Matthew 22:34–40." *Feasting on the Gospels: Matthew Vol. 2*. Louisville: Westminster John Knox, 2013.

Lucado, Max. *3:16: The Numbers of Hope*. Nashville: Thomas Nelson, 2007.

MacDonald, Gordon. "How to Spot a Transformed Christian." *Leadership Journal*, Summer 2012. https://www.christianitytoday.com/pastors/2012/summer/transformedchristian.html.

March, W. Eugene. "The Book of Haggai." *The New Interpreter's Bible*. Nashville: Abingdon, 1996.

Marsden, George M. "'Mere Christianity' Still Gets a Global Amen." *The Wall Street Journal*, March 24, 2016. https://www.wsj.com/articles/mere-christianity-still-gets-a-global-amen-1458858161.

Mary, Lawrence. "Catholic Teaching Concerning a Just War." *Catholicism*, February 21, 2006. https://catholicism.org/catholic-teaching-just-war.html.

Matera, Frank. "Galatians in Perspective: Cutting a New Path through Old Territory." *Interpretation*, July 2000, 245.

Mayfield, Tyler D. *A Guide to Bible Basics*. Louisville: Westminster John Knox, 2018.

McCann Jr., J. Clinton. "The Book of Psalms." *The New Interpreter's Bible*. Nashville: Abingdon, 1996.

McCrummen, Stephanie. "Love Thy Neighbor?" *The Washington Post*, July 1, 2017. https://www.washingtonpost.com/national/in-a-midwestern-town-that-went-for-trump-a-muslim-doctor-tries-to-understand-his-neighbors/2017/07/01/0ada50c4-5c48-11e7-9fc6-c7ef4bc58d13_story.html.

McDowell, Quinn. "Walk the Walk, Talk the Talk." *Athletes in Action*. September 16, 2020. https://athletesinaction.org/articles/walk-the-walk-talk-the-talk/.

McKim, LindaJo H. *The Presbyterian Hymnal Companion*. Louisville: Westminster John Knox, 1993.

Merry, Stephanie. "As if." *The Washington Post*, March 29, 2018. https://www.washingtonpost.com/graphics/2018/entertainment/quotable-comedies/.

Meyers, Carol L. and Eric M. *The Anchor Bible: Haggai, Zechariah 1–8*. New York: Doubleday, 1987.

Miller, Lisa. "What the Bible Really Says About Sex." *Newsweek*, February 6, 2011. https://lisaxmiller.com/what-the-bible-really-says-about-sex/4872.

Montgomery-Fate, Tom. "The memory of wilderness." *Christian Century*, April 11, 2000, https://www.christiancentury.org/reviews/2011-17/memory-wilderness?reload=1611068850601.

"Mother Teresa—Acceptance Speech." *The Nobel Prize*, December 10, 1979. https://www.nobelprize.org/prizes/peace/1979/teresa/26200-mother-teresa-acceptance-speech-1979/.

Mouw, Richard. "Getting to the Crux of Calvary." *Christianity Today*, May 2012. https://www.christianitytoday.com/ct/2012/may/getting-to-the-crux-of-calvary.html.

Northcutt, Wendy. *The Darwin Awards II: Unnatural Selection*. New York: Plume, 2003.

O'Brien, Elizabeth. "One in three Americans who get an inheritance blow it." *Market Watch*, September 3, 2015. https://www.marketwatch.com/story/one-in-three-americans-who-get-an-inheritance-blow-it-2015-19-03.

O'Connor, Kathleen M. "The Book of Lamentations." *The New Interpreter's Bible*. Nashville: Abingdon, 2001.

O'Day, Gail R. "The Gospel of John." *New Interpreter's Bible*. Nashville: Abingdon, 1995.

Orlean, Susan. "Animal action." *The New Yorker*, November 17, 2003, 92.

Bibliography

Paynter, Ben. "Showing Rescuers Where They're Needed Most." *Fast Company*, May 2018, 78.

Peterson, Eugene H. *The Message*. Colorado Springs: NavPress, 2003.

Poniewozik, James. "Twitter Lit: A New Creative Outlet." *Time*, June 3, 2010. http://content.time.com/time/magazine/article/0,9171,1993863,00.html.

Price, Reynolds. *Letter to a Man in the Fire*. New York: Scribner, 1999.

Reinicke, Carmen. "US income inequality continues to grow." *CNBC*, July 19, 2018. https://www.cnbc.com/2018/07/19/income-inequality-continues-to-grow-in-the-united-states.html.

Rosheuvel, Janis. "Let Justice Roll Down Like Waters: United Methodist Women's work for racial justice must be unceasing." *Response*, February 2017. https://www.unitedmethodistwomen.org/news/let-justice-roll-down-like-waters.

Rowles, Dustin. "20 remarkable facts you never knew about Stephen Colbert." *Salon*, April 15, 2014. https://www.salon.com/2014/04/15/20_remarkable_facts_you_never_knew_about_stephen_colbert_partner/.

Rupert, David. "Gospel on the sly." *The High Calling*, March 24, 2011. https://www.theologyofwork.org/the-high-calling/blog/gospel-sly.

Sacks, Jonathan. "Loving the Stranger." *The Office of Rabbi Sacks*, January 28, 2019. https://rabbisacks.org/loving-the-stranger-mishpatim-5779/.

"Saint in the Gutter—and Saint in Heaven." *The Nobel Prize*. https://www.nobelprize.org/prizes/peace/1979/teresa/facts/.

Sampley, J. Paul. "The First Letter to the Corinthians." *The New Interpreter's Bible*. Nashville: Abingdon, 2002.

Schuller, Eileen M. "The Book of Malachi." *The New Interpreter's Bible*. Nashville: Abingdon, 1996.

Schulte, Brigid. "How tech workers are turning to the Japanese practice of 'forest bathing' to unplug." *The Washington Post*, September 14, 2015. https://www.washingtonpost.com/news/inspired-life/wp/2015/09/14/how-tech-workers-are-turning-to-the-japanese-practice-of-forest-bathing-to-break-their-smartphone-habits/.

Smith, Eleanor. "Reinventing the wheel." *The Atlantic*, July/August 2013, 26.

"The Ebstorf Map." *This Week in Palestine*, July 2014. http://thisweekinpalestine.com/wp-content/uploads/2014/07/The-Ebstorf-Map.pdf.

"The Most Popular Bible Verses for Weddings & What They Mean." *Forever Bride*, September 30, 2019. https://foreverbride.com/inspiration/advice/most-popular-bible-verses-weddings-what-they-mean/.

Vedantam, Shankar. "The value of 'Deep Work' in an age of distraction." *Hidden Brain*, July 25, 2017. https://www.npr.org/2017/07/25/539092670/you-2-0-the-value-of-deep-work-in-an-age-of-distraction.

Vogel, Carl. "A field guide to narcissism." *Psychology Today*, January 1, 2006. https://www.psychologytoday.com/us/articles/200601/field-guide-narcissism.

Wang, Amy B. "Champion crowned at Scripps National Spelling Bee from record-breaking field." *The Washington Post*, June 1, 2018. https://www.washingtonpost.com/news/education/wp/2018/05/31/from-record-breaking-field-41-finalists-move-on-at-national-spelling-bee/.

Ward, Ed. "The Big Man Behind 'Shake, Rattle and Roll.'" *NPR Music*, October 22, 2012. https://www.npr.org/2012/10/22/163396468/the-big-man-behind-shake-rattle-and-roll.

Bibliography

Watson, Duane F. "The Letter of Jude." *The New Interpreter's Bible*. Nashville: Abingdon, 1998.

Weems, Renita. "The Song of Songs." *The New Interpreter's Bible*. Nashville: Abingdon, 1997.

Weigel, George. "Moral Clarity in a Time of War." *First Things*, January 2003, https://www.firstthings.com/article/2003/01/001-moral-clarity-in-a-time-of-war.

Weiner, Eric. "Where Heaven and Earth Come Closer," *The New York Times*, March 11, 2012, 10.

"What was the most important letter in history?" *The Atlantic*, September 2017, 104.

"What was the worst prediction of all time?" *The Atlantic*, May 2015. https://www.theatlantic.com/magazwine/archive/2015/05/the-big-question/389582/.

Wheeler, Linda. "Hope amid despair." *The Washington Post*, September 15, 2013, H8.

"Who Is the Worst Leader of All Time?" *The Atlantic*, January/February 2017, 100.

White, Jan. "Ordinary man with simple faith wrote extraordinary hymn." *The Andalusia Star-News*, November 17, 2018. https://www.andalusiastarnews.com/2018/11/17/ordinary-man-with-simple-faith-wrote-extraordinary-hymn/.

Whitman, Jake. "Power of Prayer: What Happens to Your Brain When You Pray?" *NBC News*, December 24, 2014. https://www.nbcnews.com/news/religion/power-prayer-what-happens-your-brain-when-you-pray-n273956.

"Why we're closed on Sundays." *Chick-fil-A Website*, https://www.chick-fil-a.com/about/who-we-are#:~:text=Why%20we're%20closed%20on%20Sundays&text=Having%20worked%20seven%20days%20a,a%20practice%20we%20uphold%20today.

Wilkinson, Bruce. *The Prayer of Jabez: Breaking Through to the Blessed Life*. Colorado Springs: Multnomah, 2000.

Wills, Garry. *What Jesus Meant*. New York: Viking, 2006.

———. *What Paul Meant*. New York: Viking, 2006.

Wu, Ying. "That's quite a rock." *The Wall Street Journal*, July 28, 2007, P1.

Yancey, Philip. "Grace." *Philip Yancey Website*. https://philipyancey.com/q-and-a-topics/grace.

Yee, Gale A. "The Book of Hosea." *New Interpreter's Bible*. Nashville: Abingdon, 1996.

www.ingramcontent.com/pod-product-compliance
Lightning Source LLC
Chambersburg PA
CBHW070740160426
43192CB00009B/1515